Woman, You Are Free

A Spirituality for Women in Luke

SUSAN YANOS

ST. ANTHONY MESSENGER PRESS
Cincinnati, Ohio

Nihil Obstat: Rev. Hilarion Kistner, O.F.M.
Rev. Timothy P. Schehr

Imprimi Potest: Rev. Fred Link, O.F.M.
Provincial

Imprimatur: + Most Rev. Carl K. Moeddel, V.G.
Archdiocese of Cincinnati
May 9, 2001

The *nihil obstat* and *imprimatur* are a declaration that a book is considered to be free from doctrinal or moral error. It is not implied that those who have granted the *nihil obstat* and *imprimatur* agree with the contents, opinions or statements expressed.

Cover painting by Lee Lawson, copyright ©1990
Cover design by Mary Alfieri
Book design by Sandy L. Digman

ISBN 0-86716-413-1

Published by St. Anthony Messenger Press
www.AmericanCatholic.org

Printed in the U.S.A.

To the THREE WOMEN I ADMIRE MOST
and whose own journeys
continue to inspire mine:
my mother, LADONNA,
and my daughters,
KATIE *and* ALLISON.

Contents

Introduction

Last year I was asked to speak to a gathering of women for a Sunday afternoon reflection during Advent. "You can talk about whatever you want, Susan," said the representative of the women's club who contacted me, "but I'd really like to hear you talk about Luke's views on women." One of the Bible study groups in her parish had been studying the evangelist, so she thought my talk would have particular appeal to them, as well as to a broader audience of women from throughout the deanery.

It seemed providential to me that she had suggested this topic. Luke's Gospel was my least favorite, and I rarely read the Acts of the Apostles, which he wrote as a companion piece to his Gospel. His stories of women had never seemed to me as powerfully nourishing to my spirit as, say, John's story of the Samaritan woman at the well, whose missionary zeal to speak of the man who offered her living water converted her community. Nor was Luke's description of women as appealing to me as Mark's, where the women—unlike the men—recognize the mission and identity of Jesus.

The woman of Bethany who prophetically anoints Jesus in Mark loses much in Luke's version, with its emphasis on the woman as sinner. And although Mark's Jesus assures her that wherever the Christian story is told, she will be remembered for her action, it is Luke's woman of ill repute who is more frequently remembered.

Mark (in the appended Longer Ending), Matthew and John all depict women as first to see the risen Lord. And although we know from Paul's letters that women served as leaders and missionaries in the foundling Church, Luke never mentions women as preachers or missionaries in his Acts. Under his pen, women merely occupy supporting roles (or opposing roles) to Paul's mission.

Many feminist scholars also find Luke a disturbing Gospel for women. Although there are more stories of women in Luke than in the other Gospels, the women in those stories seem to these scholars to be passive recipients of Jesus' teaching and healing. They embody the lifestyle of discipleship, but not of leadership or responsibility. Women speak less and less as the Gospel progresses, and speak very little in Acts, in which the primary female roles in the Church are to serve as hostesses for traveling missionaries and nurturers for the community. Although in Mark women are commissioned as apostles, these scholars point out, no women are commissioned in Luke. For men, in contrast, full discipleship means the power to heal, exorcise and preach.

Luke's view of the poor and oppressed was also disconcerting to me. Not that I considered myself rich—being an Indiana farmwife who raised and canned garden vegetables and sewed many of my own and my daughters' clothes over the years. Still, there was a sense of plenty in the small Hoosier community where I was raised and now live, and no abject poverty.

We grew up with all our neighbors and friends. We knew who had studied during school and who had preferred to ride around smashing mailboxes. We knew who drank too much and who was not faithful to a marriage. We knew who worked hard, who sloughed off; who saved, who bought lottery tickets. In such a community, unemployment, failed opportunities and substandard living conditions seemed less to do with oppressive social situations and more to do with willful and foolhardy decisions. Oh, of course, there were exceptions: There were true victims of illness, accidents, droughts, closed factories. All of us helped those families in any way we could. But the help was meant to be temporary, to ease them through the current crisis. We provided meals to a mother driving an injured child back and forth to physical therapy. We collected furniture, clothes and money for those burned out of their homes. We offered part-time or temporary jobs to the suddenly unemployed. We took over the spring fieldwork for a farmer fighting cancer. In each case, the community expected the individual to adapt eventually to the new situation and go on. He or she was not to become overly dependent on the community. Those who chose to remain victims failed.

Such was the attitude I acquired as a child negotiating the adult world of unspoken values and complex actions. My experience had been limited, my world small. My views remained virtually unchallenged as I married, settled down to young motherhood, farm life and a teaching position at the local community college. At the college I saw even more examples of adult students who had oppressed themselves by abusing drugs until their mental capabilities were diminished or by getting pregnant and dropping out of high school. I was empathetic with their problems and did all I could to help them achieve success. Nevertheless, I saw that those students who chose to master the situation—by taking advantage of professors' offers of help, of the college's free tutorial programs, of challenging courses and ideas—were successful. As it had been in my home community, those students who chose to remain victims failed. It never occurred to me that perhaps some do not choose such a fate or perhaps they know no other choice.

My view of the world did not change until I began seriously studying the Gospels while in my late thirties. Luke's social criticism particularly troubled me. Was I one of the oppressors, keeping others from sharing the world's plenty because I thought them unworthy, while I, of course, was worthy? Or was I, as a woman, keeping myself in the role of victim, letting my sex determine who I could be and what I could do?

Because of these questions, I knew I had to wrestle with Luke. I accepted both the invitation to speak and the proposed topic. Thus began months of research and thought. Even long after I gave the talk that icy December afternoon, I have continued to wrestle with Luke's words. It has been a very personal struggle, arising from my own feelings, attitudes, dreams, desires. What struck me as I spoke to those women was how eagerly they, regardless of age, regardless of whether they were stay-at-home moms or professional women or even mothers at all, embraced what I was saying. They asked me questions I could not answer, questions about how they, too, could be cured like the crippled woman was cured, questions which challenged my own experiences and perspectives. I spoke in metaphors (which is how Luke and Luke's Jesus speak), and they asked how to apply these metaphors to their own personal lives. No, I could not answer such questions. I still cannot, for each woman must decipher Luke's metaphors for herself.

But what that afternoon with them taught me is that I can offer my own journey into Luke. I can affirm that the journey is possible. I can affirm that Jesus will liberate. I can affirm that the seemingly impossible is possible in God. Perhaps my journey will inspire and sustain others on their personal journeys. For although we may walk along the road together, each traveler must step for herself and thus each will experience the road differently: feeling rocks underfoot where others do not feel any, or seeing beauties along the way that others are unable to see.

So this book is a rather belated attempt to say what I could not say that December afternoon. I thank the women who were there for challenging me to record my journey. I thank Father Bernard LaMontagne, Sister Ruth Eileen Dwyer, Terry Bowman, Terri Cox, Mary Alice Devor and Beth Luking for walking beside me through these many drafts. I thank April Bolton, my editor, who patiently helped shape the book into professional prose. But most of all, I thank God for the journey itself.

PART ONE

A Woman's Work Is Never Done

Chapter One

Mary, Martha and the Dishes in the Sink

> ***Activity:** Read the story of Mary and Martha (Luke 10:38-42). Imagine that you are present with Jesus in the sisters' home. With which character do you identify? Why?*

Several years ago, when my daughters were still small, I was trying to finish graduate school, teach college composition courses, play the organ at church service every Sunday morning, teach the seventh graders in our parish's religious education program, garden, sew most of the girls' clothes, volunteer at their elementary school and somehow be a farmwife and mother. As I look back on it now, I can see it was a grueling schedule, but at the time I was too immersed in it to notice the toll it was taking on my body and my spirit.

Finally in February that year, my husband had the opportunity to serve as a convention delegate for a farm organization to which he belonged. The convention was in Phoenix, and he asked me to join him. The offer of three to four days in the sun in midwinter and a chance to see Southwestern culture for the first time was just too tempting. I arranged for substitutes in my classes, solicited grandmothers to baby-sit the girls and worked ahead in my studies.

The second afternoon in Phoenix, we had some free time from the convention's meetings, so the two of us explored the streets near the convention center. We found ourselves in a chapel, kneeling beside a beautiful stained glass portrayal of the story of Mary and Martha from Luke's Gospel.

You know the story. Jesus has arrived in the hometown of the sisters Mary and Martha and has paid them an unusual honor by visiting their home to continue his teaching. Mary, in what was an unusual action for a woman of her time, sits with the men to hear Jesus' words. Martha, on the other hand, performs well the duties of a hostess in a culture that practiced lavish hospitality.

And Martha becomes angry. She is angry, as many of us would be in a similar situation, because she is doing all the work. But more than that, Martha is also shocked at Mary's mingling with a man, an outsider to the intimate family circle. Mary has broken the social taboo. It's just all too much for Martha. She complains—and is reprimanded.

The longer I studied the window that afternoon in the chapel, the more I, too, grew inexplicably angry. Here at great effort I had found time away from family and school responsibilities to attend to my other, more personal needs. Here, in this Phoenix church, I was literally, like Mary, at Christ's feet. And I was angry. Why?

For one thing, my own childhood experiences had solidified my identification with Martha. I knew her all too well. My father owned and operated a meat processing plant across from our home, and my younger sister Carolyn and I would wrap meat for him for ten cents an hour. We thought we were rich. We also thought we were a big help to him, when actually we slowed the other employees. We wasted paper, confused the various cuts of meat and generally got in their way. Dad never had enough work for both of us at once, so we took turns. I used to work there during my free time. One summer Carolyn chose to work every day. Each morning, she scurried out of the house, coming back over again to eat lunch; then right back over she went, getting out of helping with meal preparation and clearing the table and washing dishes and scrubbing the bathrooms and dusting and vacuuming the rooms. So guess who had to do all her own chores, plus Carolyn's?

I complained to Dad, with Mother's encouragement, that I deserved an increase in my allowance because I had to do double the work. He replied that Carolyn was helping him to make money; I was not. Therefore she would continue to receive her allowance plus the ten cents an hour wages. My allowance remained the same.

So for me, the story of Mary and Martha has always been about the value of women's work. Martha thought she was fulfilling her role; she even thought she was serving Christ. People have to be fed, dishes washed, the baby's diapers changed. Those things *have* to be done. Women have always seen that as their role, their mission, even, for some, their vocation. In fact, women have often turned that work into a very rich spiritual life—praying during the chores, offering the chores *as* prayer.

Martha's Message

"Why, then, is Martha reprimanded?" this young, harassed mother asked in Phoenix.

Note that in the story—a story found only in Luke, by the way—Jesus does not say to Martha, "Well, dear, I will be with you only a short time. Just throw some fruit and crackers on a plate and sit down here with your sister. We'll survive a day without a balanced meal." Instead he says, "Martha, Martha, you are anxious and worried about many things. There is need of only one thing. Mary has chosen the better part and it will not be taken from her" (10:41-42).

What is Jesus talking about? He is reprimanding Martha for more than merely complaining about her sister's lack of help. Why? Yes, I had heard those who explained that the story was about the value of a contemplative life—centered on Jesus through prayer—as opposed to an active life centered on good works. Mary was a model for all contemplatives. And I had heard those who argued that Jesus was defending Mary from the attacks of all those who would limit her. Martha loses her attempt to force Mary into the "woman's place." Yet although such explanations "worked" for me intellectually, they did not help me understand the strong emotional reaction the tale stirred within me. Why?

Most of my life, I now realize, has been a struggle to answer that question, a search for Christ in my daily experience of dirty dishes and dirty diapers. I am Martha. I suspect that many women identify with her, too. What is Luke trying to tell all of us Marthas?

Two things, I think.

1. Martha has misread the situation. She assumes that she is the host and Jesus the guest, when it is really the other way around. The Son of Man comes to serve, not to be served (Luke 22:24-27; Mark 10:45).

How have we, like Martha, misread our situations? Most of us have focused our lives on serving Christ, especially through service to others—our children, our husbands, parents, churches, schools, communities. Such good deeds are, of course, commendable. Yet, at the same time, have we not failed to understand the central message of Luke's Gospel: Jesus has brought Good News, salvation, to all? Have we not failed to understand that we are supposed to be the receptive guests at Christ's great banquet (and the banquet is a common metaphor for God's kingdom, especially in Luke)?

We know the old saying that it is better to give than to receive. As women, many of us take that saying so much to heart that we have never learned to be truly comfortable when someone gives us something of great value. I have never learned to accept compliments with ease and grace because somehow I don't feel I deserve such praise or I am vain for enjoying it. When my daughters present me with a Christmas or birthday gift that I know was expensive for them or that has taken many, many hours to make, I am somewhat uncomfortable and embarrassed. I am, of course, touched by their love, but there are so many more important things demanding their time and money. One woman told me that whenever her husband gives her an expensive gift, she wonders what it is going to cost her—either in depleted financial resources for the family because they can't really afford so expensive a gift, or in return favors he will request later. No, we are not at ease with valuable gifts. And Jesus offers us a gift that is priceless: unconditional love. We are not comfortable with that either. How can we be? We have done nothing to deserve such a gift. We are not worthy of such a gift.

And, of course, we should never request gifts. When I was a freshman in college, I asked my parents for a bathrobe to wear down to the dormitory's shower room. It seemed to them an innocent and reasonable request, especially since I argued that I needed it. However, the robe I selected was rather expensive and prettier than it was functional. Its various buttons and ties made it a rather time-consuming operation to put on, considering that I was a busy college student waiting in line to use the showers. If the truth be told, I had asked for the robe because I was embarrassed that I didn't have such nice things as my dorm companions who came from wealthier families. My parents never hesitated to make me a present of the robe, but I was later so ashamed that I had felt embarrassed by them that I rarely wore the robe. I later cut it up to make something for my own children. Now, over twenty-five years later, I am still uncomfortable asking for things. Sometimes I wish I could be a child again, sitting in my favorite chair with the J. C. Penney's catalog, putting together a Christmas list for Santa, certain that I would magically receive whatever I wanted without causing a burden for anyone. No, I don't feel worthy of priceless gifts anymore.

2. Martha has revealed her true motivation. She is so preoccupied with doing the right thing that she has done it at the expense of love. In fact, she has confused "doing the right thing" with love. For Martha, codes of behavior are ways to determine worth, value, identity. In short, she's a fussy legalist, more concerned with what she should *do* than what she should *be*.

Imagine being a guest at someone's home who tries so hard to make everything just right that you end up feeling guilty for making her go to so much trouble. One woman of my acquaintance cooks and bakes days before a holiday meal in order to include each of her children's and grandchildren's favorites. The orchestration of such a meal requires her constant vigilance. She rarely has the chance to sit down at the table before the grandchildren are finished and off to play in another room, and she is always overwhelmed with leftovers, petulantly complaining that no one ate enough. As a guest in her home, I would have much preferred fewer dishes and more of her company at the table.

Martha embarrasses her guest by showing him the trouble he is causing her and by subtly reprimanding him for not upbraiding Mary. Luke asks us to take a closer look at why we serve others. How much of what we do is done because we think that is what is expected of us? Are we fussy legalists, too? My mother told me when I was first married that a woman's housekeeping skills are judged by whether or not she has dirty dishes in the sink and unmade beds. As I write this, I notice that I have left dishes on the kitchen counter from lunch and my bed unmade. In fact, those are the two household chores I habitually slight when other jobs and interests beckon me. I cross-stitched a picture in my kitchen that reads, "A clean house means a misspent life." I refuse to let others' standards be the final judgment of my worth. (At least I try not to let others' standards determine my worth. It is, of course, far easier to say that when no one is judging me at the moment.)

If we put the Mary and Martha story back into context, we

will see that Luke associates this story with that of the Good Samaritan, which comes just before it. The Samaritan responds to an injured stranger—whom he recognizes as a despised Jew, an enemy of his people, in fact—with unquestioned compassion. Martha responds to an honored guest in her home with a sense of duty and obligation. By juxtaposing the two stories, Luke shows us the dangers of activism without love. Far too often we dehumanize the people we claim to be helping, especially if that help is institutionalized. Action without careful, critical thought leads to much of the "do-goodism" we find everywhere: acts which make us feel we have done our Christian duty of charity, but do little to build up the recipient.

Christian Action

I recall how our sixth-grade class in Catholic school formed a civics club to perform acts of service. We sold candy dishes we had enjoyed making for funds to stock a food basket for a needy family in the parish whose name had been supplied by our pastor. In our zeal, we raised enough money to fill two large boxes with bread and meat and canned goods, ignoring the pastor's admonition to "just do a little something for them." I was ever so pleased with myself and my fellow club members, especially since I had the honor of delivering the boxes. Just before Christmas, my mother drove me to the home of the needy family.

To this day, the woman's face haunts me. It held shock, embarrassment, wounded self-esteem—not the surprised look of happiness I had come to expect from reading Charles Dickens's *A Christmas Carol.* But she quietly accepted the boxes, and I quietly rode beside Mother all the way home. If the truth were told, the woman did me a service that day by not refusing the gift, by not hurting the feelings of the children who had worked to give something to her and her family—even if it was not needed or wanted. She also taught me a great deal that day about what true service is.

Writer Henri Nouwen reminds us that Christian action is not activism. Nouwen's own life was a constant, often painful, struggle to embrace a life of Christian action—the "descending" way of Jesus, as he called it—because such a life appeared in stark contrast to the upwardly mobile life so prized by the world. Nouwen left a successful university teaching career to live and work with the mentally disabled at the L'Arche Daybreak Community in Toronto, Canada. For the remainder of his life, he attempted to integrate—sometimes unsuccessfully—his gifts as spiritual writer and lecturer with his pastoral care of the L'Arche residents, some of whom were so disabled that they could not communicate with him, or even respond to his presence.

In *Lifesigns,*[1] Nouwen writes that activists want to heal, restore, redeem and re-create. However, Christians ought to point through their action to the healing, restoring, redeeming and re-creating presence of God. Activists worry about being productive, about using their time, their energy and their resources efficiently to produce the greatest effect. Christians strive to be fruitful, becoming receptive to the fruits God gives, the fruits of joy, peace, compassion, gentleness, patience, trust, self-discipline. Therefore, to an outsider Christian action looks inefficient and ineffective. Yet it reveals the solidarity of all people in God's love.

Luke's two insights in the Mary/Martha story are the focal points for the rest of our study together in this book. In Part Two, "And the Angel Came to Her," we will examine how we as women need to focus less on serving God and more on letting God serve us. That sounds weird, doesn't it? It appears to be contrary to everything we've been taught. But if we're going to step out of our Martha role, we're going to have to wrestle with this. Then in Part Three, "The Hand That Rocks the Cradle," we will examine how we can avoid being moral legalists and actually perform true acts of goodness rather than acts of do-goodism.

But before we can do that, we need first to look more closely at how Luke's Jesus relates to women.

Questions for Reflection and Discussion

- *When and how did your attitudes toward gift giving and gift receiving develop?*
- *If someone, say a coworker at Christmastime, surprises you with a gift, do you feel it necessary to reciprocate?*
- *Do you feel you have to reciprocate God's gifts to you? How?*
- *If you are a mother, how much of what you do results from your need to meet others' expectations of what a "good" mother is? How much results from your own definition of what it means to be a good mother?*
- *If you are not a mother, do you ever find yourself compelled to explain and justify why you do not have children? How do you feel about that?*
- *Relate a Gospel story that arouses in you feelings of anger. Why does it make you angry? Do you think that anger may be a call for you to face something within you or something within your current experience that needs changing?*
- *Imagine that Jesus will visit your home this evening. What is your reaction? Are you pleased, worried, excited, concerned? How would you spend the evening together? What would you do to welcome him? What do you wish he would do for you?*

Note

[1] Henri J. M. Nouwen. *Lifesigns: Intimacy, Fecundity, and Ecstasy in Christian Perspective* (Garden City, N.Y.: Doubleday, 1986).

CHAPTER TWO

Jesus: The First Women's Libber?

Activity: *The passages from Luke's Gospel and Acts listed below deal with Jesus' healing ministry to women (and his disciples who heal in his name). As you read them, answer two questions for each:*

1. *What is the social setting for Jesus' encounter with the woman? Pay particular attention to whether any taboos are involved (e.g., a woman alone in public, a man touching a woman in public, healing on the Sabbath and so forth).*
2. *What is the woman being healed of, liberated from?*

Simon's mother-in-law 4:38-39
a widow 7:11-15
a sinful woman 7:36-50
Jairus's daughter 8:40-42, 49-56
woman with a hemorrhage 8:43-48
a crippled woman 13:10-17
Tabitha Acts 9:36-41
a slave girl Acts 16:16-19

The Jewish culture generally gave women more recognition as persons than did other cultures during biblical times, but Jesus went beyond what was considered socially acceptable. Women in his culture were defined by their relationship to men and their role within the home. Women without men to protect them or women in places where they could encounter strange men were in danger of being shamed or dishonored because shame and honor were determined by external conditions, not by a person's behavior. The people of Jesus' world had a different understanding of human behavior than we do. For them, a person functioned not as an individual but as a part of a social unit. Therefore, a person depended on society to define her, and depended on society to control him. For instance, they assumed that a man could not control his physical urges when around a beautiful woman. He depended on his friends and her family to keep them apart. Likewise, they assumed a woman could not control her grief at the death of a loved one. She depended on others to keep her from throwing herself into the grave on top of the body.

When we examine Luke's Gospel, we can't help noting the "dangerous" situations Jesus puts himself in with regard to women in such a culture. Jesus enters the women's quarters, where he certainly does not belong, to heal Simon's mother-in-law and Jairus's daughter. Or he calls a woman to be where she does not belong, such as when he called the crippled woman to leave the women's section to join him in the synagogue. Or he dares to speak to the widowed woman who is without a male to define her, having lost both husband and son. Or he allows a woman to touch him in public, a woman who is ritually unclean because she is menstruating. Jesus does not hesitate to touch them, approach them, engage them in conversation. Jesus' relationship with people has nothing to do with their social situation. Jesus responds to the person, entering into a relationship with her, a relationship that empowers.

But notice that Luke does not question a woman's role in society. Immediately after Simon Peter's mother-in-law is cured, she gets up and serves her guests. Jesus gives the widow her son, and thereby her place in society is restored through a male, not through her own intrinsic worth. Paul silences the slave girl's prophetic voice, presumably because she annoyed him, and he seems unconcerned about the fact that her owners were using her for their own profit and unconcerned about her future now that she is of no profitable use to them anymore. (By the way, was the girl's prophetic gift from God or from the devil? What actually did Paul liberate her from? The abuse of her talent by her owners or an evil spirit?) For this reason, some readers complain that Jesus does not really empower women. Let's take a closer look.

Kinds of Healings

For the people in Jesus' time and place, parts of the body had symbolic meanings. In Luke's Gospel and Acts, three kinds of healings occur. Jesus heals the eyes, the body part that represented thought and understanding, and he rails about their inability to "see" correctly, to understand correctly, what he is about in his mission. Jesus says,

> *When you see a cloud rising in the west, you immediately say, "It is going to rain"; and so it happens. And when you see the south wind blowing, you say, "There will be scorching heat"; and it happens. You hypocrites! You know how to interpret the appearance of earth and sky, but why do you not know how to interpret the present time?* (12:54-56 *New Revised Standard Version Bible* [NRSV])

The eyes were also considered to be windows to the heart, so they were symbolically linked to a person's ability to choose, value and love. Therefore, the people in Jesus' generation misunderstand not because they lack sufficient knowledge, but because they have turned their trust and worth in the wrong direction. They are blind to what is true and right because of self-deception:

> *The lamp of the body is your eye. When your eye is sound, then your whole body is filled with light, but when it is bad, then your body is in darkness. Take care, then, that the light*

in you not become darkness. (11:34-35)

Jesus also heals the mouth and ears, the body parts that represented speech and self-expression—in other words, the ability to listen and respond to the truth. And he heals the trunk of the body, which, because it holds the hands and feet, represents purposeful action. When Jesus heals, he not only restores the lost function—the ability to see, to hear, to walk—but he restores the person to wholeness. The healing redefines the person: what he knows, what he understands, what he professes, what he does. The healings are not only physical but cultural, spiritual and emotional as well.

So what can we make of this? Let's examine one story, Jesus' cure of the crippled woman on the Sabbath, in order to find some clues to guide us in answering the question.

Healing the Crippled Woman

Jesus was teaching in the synagogue when he noticed a woman bent over from an affliction. Now because women were segregated from men in the synagogue, she would not have been where he was. The story does not say so, but when he calls her over to him, he is probably summoning her into an area where she is not permitted, where he is teaching, rather than meeting her later outside the building. You can feel the shock waves run through the crowd, on both sides of the screen separating the sexes. A Jewish male has singled out a woman—and in public! Jesus makes her count. Instead of discussing her case with her husband, son, brother, father or whatever man responsible for her, he turns his attention directly to her, letting her represent herself.

Then he responds to her infirmity with compassion. Because the culture assumed that her physical condition was ordained, his behavior was troubling to the community. He never asks her to explain herself, never inquires of her sins to see if this eighteen-year affliction was a just punishment. In fact, Luke doesn't tell us what has caused this affliction. It could have been disease or some terrible accident. It could have been the result of poverty and an inadequate diet and unsanitary living conditions and a daily regimen of hard work that stunted her body, her mind, her spirit. She could have been beaten by a robber, a rapist, her father or her husband. All Luke tells us is that something evil had entered her, possessed her and was trying to prevent her from being what she had been born to be.

But was the evil spirit successful? Oh yes, she is incapable of standing straight. Yes, she has endured the stares and sneers of her neighbors and family. You don't see anyone going with her to Jesus' side, do you? Most likely she has suffered greatly from physical pain, perhaps daily. Chronic pain tends to harm one's abilities to function normally, to reason fully, to respond attentively to others. Chronic pain demands chronic attention.

That is true for any oppressive burden. A demanding job can so consume a person that she has no energy or time left for family or community or even herself.

However, I would argue that in the crippled woman's case, the evil spirit has not been ultimately successful. She is, after all, present at the synagogue that day. Why? Perhaps it was because she had heard of this miracle worker who cured the sick and healed the infirm. Perhaps she just wanted to see him to see if it was true. Perhaps she hoped to touch his healing power for herself. Or perhaps she was regularly present at the synagogue every week, still able to praise God, still willing to be open to God's saving word as she heard it read, even though everyone told her that God had cursed her body. Perhaps her neighbors found her presence there a scandal—a terrible sinner punished by God—or a warning of what could happen to them if they sinned. Whatever the specific reason, we may assume that she was motivated, in part, by hope to be there. Through all her eighteen years of suffering, she had not lost hope in herself: She could still grow to full stature spiritually, if not physically. She had not lost hope in humanity: This man, she perhaps believed, would not shun her, for he ate with sinners. She had not lost hope in God, who was present to her in the midst of her pain.

Recall that Jesus says, "Woman, you are set *free*" (13:12), not "Woman, you are cured." She is free, free from whatever has bent her body: a crooked spine, psychological burdens, the law that bound her to a man, poverty, fears. Jesus the Liberator frees her.

What is it that enslaves you?

Then Jesus affirms what is good in her. He touches her—a strange woman who might be unclean—touches her in front of everyone. He makes the healing public because the bent spine has not only harmed her physically but socially. You'll recall in the story of the hemorrhaging woman, Jesus calls the crowd's attention to her so that her healing can be public, too. A complete healing requires that the woman be restored to the community that has ostracized her.

She praises God—immediately. Notice how many of the women in Luke's works respond with love and gratitude. The same cannot be said for all the men. Of the ten lepers Jesus cures, only one returns to thank him and that gratitude is his salvation (17:11-19). However, what most amazes me in this story is that the woman immediately stands straight. She trusted God. She responded to God's call. And she was freed. She stood up immediately.

Freedom to Act

Some people become so used to an affliction that they let it stunt them so that they cannot stand straight anymore, even when the affliction is gone. My youngest daughter had to wear an orthodontic brace when she was only a tiny thing in second grade in order to expand her upper palate. Before, she had been an excellent oral reader and singer and had performed a solo in the school's music program. After the visit to the orthodontist, she could barely talk around the metal bar.

She endured ridicule at school, but she nevertheless struggled to enunciate around the metal stretching across the roof of her mouth. Teachers sidestepped her in future programs in favor of her classmates who could speak more clearly. When the bar was finally removed, she continued to speak as if it were still there. Eight years later, she is still sometimes difficult to understand. And despite vocal lessons and praise from her teacher, she refuses to perform publicly.

Liberation means more than a mere removal of the affliction. It means being free of the crippling effects on our spirit as well. That requires our cooperation and participation. We have to be able to envision a life beyond our affliction. More importantly, we have to realize that we have the potential to attain that life even with our affliction.

However, the leader of the synagogue is deeply troubled by Jesus' action. Rather than blame Jesus, he blames the woman. Yet she is totally innocent. She did not call out to Jesus; she did not petition to be cured. Jesus called her. But the leader's logic has it that because she was present there that day, she caused Jesus to see her (just as women were found at fault and considered unclean because of normal biological functions, such as menstruation and childbirth). Jesus' words slash through the cruelty and hypocrisy of the synagogue's leader who cannot see what the rules have done to women, who cannot see that a woman is more valuable than an ox or an ass, more valuable than the service she performs. The leader cannot see that a woman is a person, too. Jesus calls her a "daughter of Abraham," a title virtually unknown in Jewish writing, although "son of Abraham" can be found. He is reminding her and the community that she is also an heir to God's promise of salvation.

Because of the belief of that culture that honor and shame were determined by external circumstances—by sex or social position or physical condition, for instance—Jesus' healing of women in the area of the trunk, which symbolizes purposeful action, takes on particular significance. Sex, social position and physical condition are all a matter of birth and cannot be changed (in their world!). Therefore, a person's position, they concluded, must also be fixed and unchangeable—ordained by God. Jesus challenges this conclusion.

For women, a restoration to wholeness means they must be cured of their inability to act purposefully. But because Jesus does not question a woman's role in society, as we saw, this ability to act purposefully must go beyond mere social organization or social expectations and limitations of women. It must go beyond the external constraints to the internal ones. Recall the Exodus story of the people in the desert. God freed them from Egypt, but they still thought, ate, worked and feared like slaves. Time and time again, God provided opportunities for the people to give up their attitude of servitude to become truly free, but they complained, longed for the food of Egypt, ran from adversaries, cowered and groveled. God did not want slaves in the Promised Land. A new kingdom demanded a new people. So God waited until the slaves died, and their children, born in freedom and trained in the responsibilities and demands of freedom, took possession of Canaan.

This is, perhaps, the message of Luke's works as well. Merely changing the external situation will not truly and completely heal these women. They must first be healed interiorly. They must first understand that they have worth and dignity as daughters of God, that who they are is of more value than what they do. If their action is to be purposeful, it must spring forth from the center of their being, a center focused upon God, accepting of Jesus and ready to do God's will as they are led by the Spirit.

Questions for Reflection and Discussion

- *How has our culture defined what you do?*
- *Have you ever felt that being a woman prevents a person from doing something, being something, she wants? If you*

have had such an experience, what was it you wanted to do or be? How did being a woman stop you? What was your response?

- *Describe an experience with suffering—whether it was your suffering or that of someone you know, whether the suffering was physical or social or emotional. What was the experience like? What thoughts and feelings occurred? How was reality different during that time? How did the experience of suffering alter how you or this person you know relate to others?*
- *How does our culture respond to suffering?*
- *How does our Christian faith enlighten us to respond to suffering?*
- *What would you like to remember from the story of the crippled woman the next time you must endure suffering?*

PART TWO

And the Angel Came to Her

Chapter Three

Luke's Quiet Revolution

> ***Activity:*** *Read the story of the Pharisee and the tax collector (18:9-14), and the stories of Jesus' visit to Zacchaeus (19:1-10) and Paul's visit to Ephesus (Acts 19:1-40). For these individuals to accept Jesus, what had to occur? If they did not accept Jesus, why not?*

Luke's persistent theme is that God is a merciful benefactor who heaps benefits upon us without regard to moral performance. We just saw that in action in the healing stories of women. These women were considered by their communities to be sinful, unclean, taboo, undeserving of a good man's intentions. But Jesus showered them with healing gifts.

Several of Jesus' parables underscore this same theme: the lost sheep (15:3-7), the lost coin (15:8-10) and the lost son (15:11-24)—the last one a parable found only in Luke. What is lost seems worthless to Jesus' audience, but the actions of the characters in the parables force the hearers to reestablish the worth of all creation in God's eyes. The shepherd leaves the ninety-nine in the flock, risking their safety to predators or thieves or the elements, to rescue and restore one sheep. No savvy businessman would take such a foolhardy risk. The woman leaves other, surely we would say more important, pursuits to look for a coin, burning precious oil to do so. And when she finds it, she calls in the town for a celebration—for a coin! How ridiculous, we would say! The father receives back his son who has squandered his inheritance, shamed his family (remember the code of honor of the people) by deserting their ways and insulted the father by demanding the inheritance before the father's death. The son is not truly repentant, what with his plan to return home to get better food, not to seek reconciliation, and his memorized speech, which he hopes will appease the old man. Yet, without waiting to hear his son's speech, the father joyfully restores him to his rightful place in the family (which some readers interpret to be that which has been lost in this parable). This will never work, we say. This will never teach the boy respect or the price one must pay for behavior. This defies all logic. No one acts this way. Only God acts this way.

How can we respond to this God, a God who gives grace regardless of what we do? A God who accepts us back like the father embraced his prodigal son? A God who, even after we crucified Jesus, resurrected him and gave him back to us—all forgiven? This kind of God is, well, an absolute fool. No one acts like that because to do so would make one vulnerable to others who would, perhaps, take advantage of that vulnerability. This kind of God is truly awesome. This kind of God is thoroughly and completely liberating.

So how are we to respond to such a radical freedom? For Luke, the only acceptable answer is a revolution of our minds. Nothing else will do. The change must be that radical and that pervasive.

Most of us tend to evaluate others and ourselves by external traits or events. Yet Luke shows that we cannot use our actions and behavior as a measuring stick to evaluate our relationship with God. Something more is at stake. In the story of the Pharisee and the tax collector, Luke makes this point forcefully.

The Pharisee and the Tax Collector

A common interpretation of the parable of the tax collector and the Pharisee has it that the Pharisee was self-righteous, crowing before God while holding others in contempt, while the tax collector was honest in his dealings with God. However, if Luke did not introduce the story by having Jesus rebuke the Pharisee for self-righteousness, his listeners would have found nothing reprehensible in the man. He is, by the standards of the Temple, a pious Jew. He offers God a prayer of thanksgiving for bestowing such favor on him that he has not been led into sin. He is grateful for being chosen as one of God's own, not like all the other men, not like that tax collector there who proves by his sinful actions that he cannot be one of the elect. He stands in God's presence, the normal attitude for prayer in the Temple, not a sign of his arrogance, as I had been taught. He follows the commandments. He goes beyond the proscribed religious obligations for fasting and almsgiving. His behavior is completely consistent with what one would expect from a devout believer. Similarly, the tax collector's behavior in the Temple is consistent with what one would expect from a sinner.

Tax collectors were notorious for their corrupt practices—at least that is how they were perceived to be by those who paid the taxes. The Romans gave them free rein in the collection of the required monies, so many overcharged the subjects, pocketing the excess. No one could prove it, of course. It was all legal, of course. Yet many tax collectors grew wealthy while small landowners lost their land. Therefore, they were doubly hated: first, for cooperating with the despised Romans and the tremendous burden the Romans placed on their subjected peoples to finance the empire, and second, for their suspected dishonesty and greediness at the expense of their own countrymen. The tax collector in our story seems to be aware of his status. His attitude in prayer is the attitude of one who is in mourning—beating his breast, head downcast. He mourns for what is not his: God is not concerned with the likes of him; God's kingdom is not for him; God's covenant was not made with men like him; God's promises are not for him. He is an outcast, a failure. His occupation and position in society spell this out all too clearly. Nothing he can do will change that. He seems to be without hope, in utter despair, completely and irrevocably lost.

So how can Jesus say that when the tax collector returned home, he was justified while the Pharisee was not? The tax collector's despair prevents him from making an outward sign of conversion. He makes no reparation for his past deeds. Nowhere in the story are we told that from then on he dealt honestly with others. We are confused. We see nothing to emulate in the tax collector's life, yet we are told not to emulate the Pharisee who has led an upright life in the sight of all believers. How, then, can we judge others' actions?

Ah, there's the point. We cannot. Luke argues that it is not what we do that matters, but who we are. It is not the code of behavior we have accepted, but the core of our being. If God is at the core, all is well regardless of external circumstances. If our egos are at the core, all is lost. Unfortunately, most of us are like the Pharisee: We never examine the core to see what we have allowed to rule there. Jesus praises the tax collector because even though the religious authorities have made him feel that God is lost to him, he continues to grieve for God's presence. And he is justified. God *is* present. That is why Jesus identifies his mission as preaching the Good News of God's salvation to all, including the likes of just this tax collector, to individuals who pine for God, even when the established religious codes deny them entry and participation in the Temple culture.

Therefore, acceptance of Jesus, an outcast and failure who associated with outcasts and failures, requires that we really, deeply probe ourselves. To do that requires that we determine whatever it is that robs us of our true identity as God's daughters, which prevents us from fulfilling God's will for us, which reduces us from persons to things. Two steps are necessary.

Recognizing What Has Limited Us

First, we must recognize the sins that have limited and enslaved us. Zacchaeus, another tax collector in Luke's Gospel, is both surprised and honored by Jesus' visit to his home. Zacchaeus's neighbors are both surprised and shocked, for what would a holy man want with such a sinner—ah, that is, presuming Jesus really is a holy man. During the course of the meal, Zacchaeus, moved by God's love for him as revealed in this human guest sitting at his table, suddenly realizes that it is not his stature which has stunted him, but his lifestyle, a lifestyle which has deprived him of his real identity as a son of Abraham, an heir to the covenant, and which has made him a mere tax collector. Immediately he repents of his sins and vows to be a very different man. He is still a tax collector; externally his situation has not changed. However, internally, he is a changed man, a converted man. He has abandoned his old perspective and adopted a new one. And that is what "conversion" means. The word itself derives from "worth," so conversion is a turning around, a turning back to one's true value. It is a change, a becoming of that which we had always been meant to be. (For another perspective on this story, see Malina and Rohrbaugh, *Social-Science Commentary on the Synoptic Gospels,* 385-387. They argue that Zacchaeus's heart is in the right place and thus not in need of conversion, which is why Jesus visits him. However, the community has labeled him a sinner because of the source of his wealth. Jesus' visit restores or heals him in the eyes of his neighbors.)

Women who follow Luke's admonition and probe themselves for the sins that limit and enslave them must be alert and wary. Female spiritual directors, sociologists and psychologists who have studied and worked with women warn us that our socialization process prompts us to different vices than men have. Because most religious texts were written by men, and most confessors and many spiritual directors are male, women are often admonished to beware of temptations which predominantly plague men, not the temptations which plague primarily women. Men struggle against pride, aggression, disobedience to lawful authority, self-assertion. For women, just the opposite is true. We struggle against a *lack* of these very attitudes. Instead of pride, we tend toward a submersion of personal identity; instead of aggression, we acquiesce into submissiveness and passivity; instead of disobedience, over-dependence; and instead of self-assertion, self-hatred. These vices may express themselves in our behavior as timidity that makes us easily manipulated. Or perhaps we are self-absorbed and small-minded. Women often struggle against fear—a fear of the world outside which threatens the security of their domestic circle, and a fear of recognizing their own competence as women (which may also threaten the security of the domestic circle). Women's lives are often characterized by "drifting"; they often seem to move through occupations and pursuits without purpose or direction, constantly reacting to situations others control, abandoning personal dreams and goals for the dreams and goals of significant others in their lives—parents, husband, children. Sometimes women live vicariously through the lives of those they love, identifying themselves through their children's accomplishments, for instance.

The theologian Elizabeth Johnson in her work *She Who Is: The Mystery of God in Feminist Theological Discourse* argues that far too many women are captivated by the myth of Sleeping Beauty. We lie passive and silent in a hundred-year sleep, waiting for the lover's kiss to revive us, to set us free, to define us and give us meaning as his bride. He, meanwhile, is off having adventures, discovering and maturing in his identity in the quest.

When will we fully awaken to our own true worth?

Recognizing Contradictory Loyalties

The second step in our move to accept Jesus is to recognize contradictory loyalties. "Every kingdom divided against itself will be laid waste," Jesus warns, "and house will fall against house" (11:17). Luke's description of Ephesus is of a kingdom divided. Many came to believe after hearing Paul's preaching and witnessing Paul's healings, but they hung on to their magic books. They trusted God, yes, but not enough to abandon their own attempts to manipulate and control events. No spiritual growth was possible until they burned their magic books. The silversmiths in the city also experienced dissension from contradictory loyalties. Belief in this Christ would harm their livelihood, which consisted of making statues for the pagan goddess Artemis. What will it be? Faith in Jesus or in the pocketbook? Faith in Jesus or in worldly success and fame? Faith in Jesus or in our own magic spells and good luck charms?

I remember being so frustrated as a child with the girls presented to me in children's stories (I grew up before the age of multicultural textbooks) that I turned in disgust to the romanticized tales of Wild West outlaws. My favorite was Johnny Ringo, mainly because I liked the name, for I knew next to nothing about his life. So I became Johnny Ringo in my imagination. When I later learned how disturbing and unromantic the West really was, I still clung to Johnny, but he grew in stature from a lowly outlaw to a whaling captain or a rebel soldier or a desert prince or whatever I happened to be reading at the time. Over the years, I turned to Johnny whenever I couldn't be or do what I wanted. When I couldn't stand up to the girl bullying me at school, Johnny stood up to traitors within his kingdom. When I couldn't go camping without my parents like my male cousins did all the time, Johnny led a tracking party through the frozen wilderness. Unfortunately, Johnny was always more interesting than I was—and still is. Escaping into his world prevented me from facing the young woman I was growing into. She was always waiting through her childhood and adolescent sleep for Johnny to somehow spark her to life.

You can imagine how this inner yearning affected my self-identity over the years. I had little respect for women as achievers. My favorite authors, my favorite teachers, my favorite historical figures were all men. I preferred the company of men. Part of my spiritual struggle has been to cultivate female friendships and to accept women as competent and capable individuals. And I have had to recognize the divided loyalties which have resulted in dissension in my "home": I have had to send Johnny Ringo packing, oust him from the premises and accept myself as a woman.

My experience, unfortunately, is familiar to many women, especially well-educated ones. Some women dislike and distrust their female peers, finding that women often become complaining and "catty" in the face of competition while men increase their competitive spirit and output. Some do not admire their female supervisors, finding that women bosses frequently feel threatened and intimidated by their subordinates. Some are uncomfortable with female ministers of the Eucharist, female preachers or pastors, believing that women are unworthy or inappropriate representatives of God. Some are uncomfortable with ascribing feminine attributes to God, rejecting any but a male divinity, and, in a sense, alienating themselves from the Divine.

Retrieving Lost Gardens

For that reason, several contemporary women authors argue in their works that a woman cannot accept herself until she accepts other women, cannot know her own value until she can recognize the value of other women, cannot come into possession of her own talents until she acknowledges the talents of other women. Nor can she understand her own history until she reclaims the history of her sisters, her grandmothers, her mother. When she does so, she will discover the indomitable spirit behind the seemingly insignificant details of many women's lives. For instance, so many "trivial" feminine pursuits—such as gardening, quilting, volunteer service, herb lore—were frequently the only outlets available for our female ancestors to express their intelligence, power and creativity. In the eighteenth-century utopian community at New Harmony, Indiana, women found release from their bleak, utilitarian surroundings by creating intricately quilted coverlets. The community's male authorities found all this delicate stitching to be a sign of vanity, if not a waste of time, and put a stop to it, sending the women back to their chores. So much for a female utopia!

Novelist Alice Walker, appalled at the dearth of Black women artists, converted her anger at Black women for failing to "succeed" into a celebration of how her female predecessors cultivated their artistic talents by other means. *In Search of Our Mothers' Gardens* records her own mother's indomitable spirit, which refused to allow poverty and oppressive work to be the defining factors of her life. Despite the long hours Walker's mother worked just to keep the family clothed and fed, despite the many disappointments and sorrows of her life, with every move the family made, she transformed their bleak yard into a profusely blooming garden. Walker, in recovering her mother's story, absorbed not just the beauty within the struggle of her mother's life, but the creative spark that guided it as well. "Guided by my heritage of a love of beauty and a respect for strength," she writes, "in search of my mother's garden, I found my own."[1]

We must make the effort to retrieve those lost gardens from the weeds of neglect that choke them. In the process, we will discover not only how lovingly the gardens were once tended, but how loving is our effort to retrieve them.

For a woman cannot love herself until she can love other women.

If a woman is to achieve this kind of love, she must undertake much soul searching and much repentance for past attitudes. Yes, Luke's Jesus calls for repentance. But this kind of repentance is not a mere tabulation of all actions we have sinfully committed or omitted. Rather it is a call to drop the line and sound the depths of our hearts, our minds. It is a call for a quiet revolution.

The price of such a revolution will be great. Jesus insists that we clearly understand the costs before we proceed:

> *For which of you, intending to build a tower, does not first sit down and estimate the cost, to see whether he has enough to complete it? Otherwise, when he has laid a foundation and is not able to finish, all who see it will begin to ridicule him, saying, "This fellow began to build and was not able to finish." Or what king, going out to wage war against another king, will not sit down first and consider whether he is able with ten thousand to oppose the one who comes against him with twenty thousand? If he cannot, then, while the other is still far away, he sends a delegation and asks for the terms of peace. So therefore, none of you can become my disciple if you do not give up all your possessions.* (14:28-33)

Which possessions are you clinging to: passivity? timidity? over-dependence? self-absorption? small-mindedness? fear? self-hatred?

Revolutions are painful. People are beheaded; cities burned; children slaughtered. Revolutions are shocking. Hidden motives are revealed; festering hatreds exposed. Revolutions are dangerous. Trusted friends may just turn out to be foes; what we thought valuable may prove worthless and what worthless, valuable. Revolutions are convulsive. Walls are breached; prisons and ghettoes unlocked; sewers and cellars and torture chambers flushed, releasing all manner of diseased and deformed creatures. If we are not careful, we may be swallowed up by this mob: swallowed by anger, bitterness, rage, despair. We may even be crucified.

Yet the Jesus in Luke's writings calmly and forcefully calls you to the most important, painful, shocking, dangerous and convulsive revolution of your life. Jesus calls you to be the person God means you to be. Yes, you, a woman crippled by the sins of self-hatred and passivity and over-dependence and non-identity that have stunted you. You, a woman bent over by divided loyalties at war within you. Leave where you are, come here to the community and stand up straight.

You have been called. Will you respond? It's time to revolt against things as they are now, revolt against the person you have let yourself become. It's time to stand up straight.

Questions for Reflection and Discussion

- *What were your favorite fairy tales? How did they depict women, especially the young heroine? How did they influence your conception of yourself as a woman?*
- *Who were your role models as you were growing up? What characteristics attracted you to them? Why were these characteristics important?*
- *Who are your role models today? If your role models have changed over the years, how does that signify a change in you?*
- *When you were an adolescent, what were the goals, dreams and plans you had for your future? Are you pursuing them today? If not, why did you abandon them?*
- *What kinds of relationships do you have with women? Are they satisfying? Why or why not?*
- *What kinds of relationships do you have with men? Are they satisfying? Why or why not?*
- *How much do you know of the stories of your female ancestors? Do you possess any of their handiwork, belongings, photographs? What happened to the homes they established and nurtured? Where can you begin to*

recover the details of their lives? How can you preserve these stories for future women in your family?

Note

[1] Alice Walker. *In Search of Our Mothers' Gardens: Womanist Prose* (New York: Harcourt, 1974), p. 243.

Chapter Four

Women at the Cross

Activity: *Using whatever medium you prefer—clay, paint, chalk, colored pencils, fabric, yarn—express what Jesus' call to conversion means to you in your life. One woman I know shaped a clay female figure emerging from stone. One arm and both legs are still trapped, but the rest of the body strains away from the rock. The figure is powerful and muscular and determined, and reveals the sculptor's struggle for spiritual liberation and the pain it causes her. Another woman drew tablets similar to what are often pictured for the Ten Commandments. On one she wrote, "Be perfect." On another, "Be great." A jagged line courses down the center of each tablet, splitting them into fragmented pieces, signifying that she must break the world's hold on her definition of herself and of success.*

On occasion I have the responsibility and joy of teaching a course on women and literature at the university where I work. This course is a particular joy for me because I discover each time how gifted many of these writers are. Given my previous preference for male writers, the experience has been like stumbling upon a forgotten trunk in my grandmother's attic—all covered with dust and cobwebs on the outside, but inside full of beautiful laces and love letters and photographs of family members I thought lost to us. The course is also a responsibility, because most of the students who sign up for it are women, and I know that their growth as scholars, as future writers and as individuals will in part depend on their ability to assess both the strengths and the weaknesses of these authors' visions.

Because many of my students are older women with husbands or ex-husbands and children, the authors who speak most profoundly to them deal with the struggle of a woman to integrate her inner person and desires with her outer roles and relationships. Two authors who never fail to arouse strong reactions are Kate Chopin and Adrienne Rich.

In Chopin's novel *The Awakening,* the main character, Edna, attempts to integrate herself fully, to satisfy the basic, yet often conflicting, desires for love and for a sense of belonging with the desire for autonomy. No other female character in the book is able to integrate the three desires. They either deny autonomy in order to be wife and mother, or deny love in order to follow a personal goal, such as to be a musician. Therefore, my students ardently wish Edna to succeed where the other characters fail, to find fulfillment as wife, mother, woman. Yet her decisions frustrate us. She comes to see that to have her own way means that she must hurt others, most especially her children, and that she will not do. Yet, to avoid hurting them, she must hurt herself, which she also now finds intolerable. As she sees it, the only way to gain total independence is by ceasing to exist: If she cannot attain full existence, then she chooses not to exist at all. My students will not accept her final decision. Some of my students are angry with the ending, because they desperately want her to show them how they can successfully juggle these desires to be wife, mother and woman into a fully integrated existence. One divorced mother of three adolescent sons told me she was so angry with Edna that she threw the book against the wall.

Other students see Edna as self-indulgent, neglecting her children and her husband, and they completely reject her and Chopin's book—as did many of Chopin's contemporaries, who banned the book and ultimately silenced her as a writer.

So is it selfish to want a full existence? Is it even possible to have one?

The second author who evokes a strong response is Adrienne Rich, especially her poem "Snapshots of a Daughter-in-Law." My female students identify with the young woman of the poem who, like Edna, fails to find older women who can serve as adequate role models to guide her through the struggle to negotiate between the role she desires (to be the poet) and the role she feels compelled to perform (to be the wife and mother). She angrily rejects the lifestyle of her mother-in-law, but cannot yet find her own way. As she goes about her housework, she hears voices within her mind that encourage her to be different. Both infatuated with and appalled by the inner urges she feels—the inner voices calling her—she stands at the kitchen sink or stove, lost in thought, absent-mindedly allowing the running water to become so hot it scalds her arm, or the match she holds burn so low it scorches her thumbnail. Dare she entertain these thoughts? Dare she act on them? The voices tell her to do the exact opposite of what every good girl has been taught: Have no patience, be insatiable, save yourself. But isn't this pure selfishness and egoism? Are these the voices, she asks, of angels or of monsters? Is she being led toward salvation or damnation? Or is it damnation to ignore them, silence them? She can't decide. But she is willing to call them angels, for she is already miserable, trapped in a world not of her making. Nothing else could possibly make things worse.

These two works are powerful ones for me as well, for like Edna in the novel and the young woman in the poem, I don't know if that small voice within, calling me to be more than I am, calling me to leave my place in the synagogue and come over to this strange man reputed to work miracles, is an angel leading me to greater peace or a monster leading me into the hell of selfish egoism. Wouldn't it be safer, better, to remain where I am, even if to do so would mean that I remain crippled?

Luke is the only one of the four evangelists to present us with another young woman who heard those voices: Don't be afraid, accept the power, you have it within you if you but say yes, if you but acknowledge it (1:26-38). Since she listened, accepted and believed what those voices told her, salvation history has never been the same. She became pregnant with hope, pregnant with life and love, pregnant with Jesus, her salvation.

Being Open to Development

Do you remember when you or a friend were pregnant? We pampered ourselves when we gave birth to our children, when we co-created with God a life. We watched our diet, eating healthy foods and taking vitamins. We exercised, bought (or borrowed) a whole new wardrobe, allowed others to give us baby showers. We accepted the kindness of strangers who offered us seats in crowded places or picked up things for us we dropped in the store. We read books and consulted the wisdom of our mothers, aunts, older sisters. We created an external womb: a nursery with a crib, tiny booties, snuggly sleepers. We pampered ourselves because we knew that the better care we took of ourselves, the better chance that new life within us had of developing and growing into birth.

When have you pampered yourself to give birth to a dream? To co-create with God an idea, a project, a vision, your spirit? Why is it that we are so reluctant to pamper ourselves to give birth to our very selves?

The reason is that it sounds selfish.

The traditional view of Mary has done much to teach us that pampering ourselves for our own development is selfish.

Mary is often considered as submissive, passive, self-effacing, compliant. Many readers of Luke's Gospel think that Jesus criticizes her motherly instincts to preserve her family, maintain the status quo, keep Jesus safe. The child Jesus rebukes her for frantically searching for him when he was preaching in the Temple (2:49). The adult Jesus seems to deny her special claim on him. When told while he is teaching that his family want to see him, he responds: "My mother and my brothers are those who hear the word of God and act on it" (8:21). Later, when a woman in the crowd cries out, "Blessed is the womb that carried you and the breasts at which you nursed," Jesus responds, "Rather, blessed are those who hear the word of God and observe it" (11:27-28). Mary suffers quietly, keeping things in her memory or treasuring them in her heart (2:19, 51), never openly confronting or questioning her pain. One can imagine how she suffered in her attempts to grapple with the meaning of the Incarnation.

All mothers are bewildered by their children's growth into maturity and selfhood. How much more so for the mother of God. And while the other evangelists give Mary a more prominent role at the crucifixion, Luke remains strangely silent about her then. She appears nowhere in the account of Jesus' final hours. After Jesus' death, she seems to have no particular prominence in the fledgling Church community either. Although many paintings picture her as present at the Ascension and in the upper room at Pentecost, Luke's account is not so clear or precise (Acts 1:1-14 and 2:1-4). He does not specifically describe Mary as being present at the events, only at her being with the disciples during prayer. We assume the rest.

Some women have chosen to reject the biblical tradition, feeling this is the only way to achieve spiritual maturity. For after all, spiritual development is a form of human development and the model for human development is to reject conformity and role expectations in favor of greater autonomy. But before we completely reject Luke's writings, perhaps we should first look at the notion of "self." If we are to take up our cross daily, deny the self, then we must first know what it is that we are denying.

Locating the Self

For women, that is a particularly poignant and troubling problem. Joann Wolski Conn, a writer, spiritual director and professor of religious studies, writes:

> *Women spending themselves on their family, their students, patients, or members of their religious community often have low self-esteem, and thus their emotional dependency makes them subtly very demanding on others for appreciation and adulation. Their inability to be assertive and their lack of self-worth can result in covert manipulation, pretended helplessness, evasion of conflict situations. Their desire for peace at any price has a high cost: repression of anger can result in bouts of depression. On the other hand, behavior that is criticized as not virtuous, as selfish or immature (e.g., a mother leaving small children in the care of others so that she can pursue an interesting job even though there is no severe financial need, or a member of a religious community questioning her superior's judgment about the appropriateness of an assignment) can be the behavior of a woman whose self-worth is more secure, who is less emotionally dependent and, thus, less demanding and less manipulative in her relationships.*[1]

The problem for me and for many of the women with whom I have worked in my teaching and ministry is that we have no concept of self to deny. University teachers working with older students have become aware that when their students drop out, the reasons are often difficult to understand. Most students drop out because of lack of achievement—earning bad grades, for instance. But an alarming number of female students drop out just when they achieve success, just when they begin to earn good grades. The family perceives the woman's success as a threat. The husband fears that she won't need him anymore, or that she will find him uninteresting. The children are afraid that Mother will change so much that she won't be Mother anymore. One student I know arrived home after classes one day to find that her husband had packed her bags and had them at the door ready for her. "You're not the woman I married," he said. "I don't know who you are anymore."

Is that what it means to carry the cross: to withdraw from classes because the family cannot adjust to Mother's growth? Or would a better response be for Mother to creatively help her family grow along with her? Perhaps the second option is a better understanding of what it means to carry the cross. The cross is not and should never become a symbol of victimization and oppression. Rather the cross is a symbol of creative suffering which, when embraced, transforms and redeems all around. To become a full disciple, to become the person God calls us to be will most likely provoke opposition from others, for our lives then become a challenge to others to become the people they are meant to be, as well. Jesus' life most certainly provoked opposition. Yet Jesus' refusal to abandon his own personal integrity and faithfulness to God in the face of death transformed even those who died beside him (23:39-43), even those who crucified him (23:47).

Often when women define self-denial as self-effacement, they provoke resentment in their families, not love. Rather than freely giving the self to others, we actually withhold the self, giving instead what we think the other needs or wants. What others really want is the gift of our wisdom, our talents, our labor, our presence, our love. They also want our tears and our brokenness, because it is often in our brokenness that we become most present to another. What others really want is *us*.

Making Choices

So when Jesus tells the woman in the crowd that it is more blessed to be his disciple than his mother (11:27-28), he is not denigrating his mother, but uplifting all women. We are not determined by our biological functions, Jesus is saying, but by our individual choices. Remember that Mary was the first disciple, the first to choose to say "yes." The Spirit comes upon her, overshadowing and filling her, dwelling within her as if she were now the Ark of the Chosen People, a new temple of God (1:35). Each of us is to be that temple. Each of us is to make God present to the world.

My oldest daughter, Katie, is particularly fond of pumpkin pie. In fact, it's one of the few desserts this girl who was born without a sweet tooth will eat. (I know. It's a strange child who doesn't like dessert!) One evening at the supper table, after everyone had had a serving of pie, there was one small slice left in the pan. As our children (all daughters) had been taught to do when they were about to take the last of something (because it was what my mother had taught my sister and me), Katie asked if anyone else would like a second helping. The other family members refused, as did I. But there must have been something in my manner that tipped her off that, yes, I really would have liked another piece, even though I didn't say so, and I was willingly sacrificing it to her. Perhaps I hesitated before responding or made some gesture. "Are you sure, Mom?" Again I refused. "You can have it, Mom." Still I refused, getting a little aggravated by this time. Finally, she sighed, took her knife, sliced the piece down the middle, and slid one tiny half onto my plate. "Quit being a mother," she said, "and say what you really want."

I once told this story to a group of women who gave me the third degree afterwards—albeit politely. They questioned me about why I had taught the girls to ask if anyone else wanted what they wanted. I thought I was teaching them to share, just as my mother had taught me to share. However, these women led me to realize that if my daughters were truly sharing, they would from the first offer to do just what my daughter had eventually done—break the whole into parts for all (sound like the Eucharist?). Instead of asking whether anyone else would like a second helping, the girls should ask whether anyone would like to share a piece with them. Notice that the second offer is much more inviting, welcoming the other into fellowship instead of offering to slavishly serve the other person. Rather than teaching them to share, I had, in fact, been teaching my daughters, as a matter of course, to give away completely and entirely and irrevocably to another what they truly wanted or desired. Was that self-denial or self-effacement? Would such actions foster love or resentment? Fortunately, Katie saw things differently and taught me a valuable lesson that day.

These lessons are difficult for many women to learn because of how they were acculturated as girls. The East Asian cultures have long known that a healthy person possesses both *yin* (feminine qualities of softness, tolerance, receptivity, mercifulness, withdrawal) and *yang* (masculine qualities of strength, judgment, independence, aggressiveness, activity). However, here in the West, women have, at times, been encouraged to be solely feminine. If to be a healthy adult means that we accept both sides of our personality, what does a woman do in a culture that may criticize and punish her for having "masculine" thoughts and feelings? Mary Pipher, a clinical psychologist who has worked with troubled adolescents, writes in *Reviving Ophelia:*

> *Girls have long been trained to be feminine at considerable cost to their humanity. They have long been evaluated on the basis of appearance and caught in myriad double binds: achieve, but not too much; be polite, but be yourself; be feminine and adult; be aware of our cultural heritage, but don't comment on the sexism. Another way to describe this femininity training is to call it false self-training. Girls are trained to be less than whom they really are. They are trained to be what the culture wants of its young women, not what they themselves want to become.*[2]

Personal Self and Public Self

Our culture may split girls into two selves: a true one that is the personal self, and a false one that is the public self. Some girls quickly learn that only the false side can be revealed, and the false self needs constant validation from the outside to determine whether it is indeed meeting the standards of femininity. The true self must be suppressed, denied or rejected. Many women end up living a lie.

One of the first novelists to explore this dichotomy in female personality was Charlotte Brontë. Before the publication of *Jane Eyre* in 1847, novels had concentrated on the social ethic in which the imperative for women is their responsibility to the community and the gauge of their spiritual health is how well they perform their duty to others. Brontë offered an alternative: The imperative for her female characters is responsibility to *self* and the gauge of their spiritual health is personal integrity. Therefore, Brontë's *Jane Eyre* is characterized by deep divisions, which are often represented as pairs of contrasting characters. For instance, the mad wife imprisoned in the attic may be said to represent Jane's repressed passionate and sexual feelings. In this interpretation, mad Bertha is Jane's alter ego, an identity that her religious beliefs and society's strictures have forced her to lock up deep within. But like Bertha, who escapes from the attic and sets fire to Jane's bed the night before Jane's wedding, these feelings threaten to erupt violently. Jane's survival depends on her ability to mediate between the conflicting, and potentially destructive, extremes of passion and repression, reason and feeling, reality and imagination, duty and rebellion. She—and every woman—has two crucial lessons to learn: self-control *and* self-assertion. She must learn that self-control is not mere repression but a complex balance of impulses that remain fundamentally true to self.

For many girls, this battle between the selves begins in earnest with puberty and the casualties may be great.

However, minor skirmishes may occur much earlier. Some researchers have posited that elementary school teachers interact with boys more often than with girls. Just one example: Boys are often allowed to call out answers in the classroom while girls are admonished to raise their hands before they speak. By high school, the self-esteem of some girls has plummeted, especially when compared to that of boys.

To become an authentic person means that we own all of our experiences, emotions, passions, desires, thoughts and feelings. Yet, too often, girls are not allowed to do so, and find that they must sacrifice half of themselves on the altar of public approval. Interestingly enough, Brontë's *Jane Eyre* was criticized by her contemporaries for being an "anti-Christian" novel. Readers were appalled at what they considered Jane's pride, ingratitude and refusal to submit to her social destiny. But what most appalled them was Jane's anger at the strictures of society that prevented her from integrating her complete self.

Men, too, struggle to integrate their feminine and masculine aspects, and often they, too, find this struggle painful and debilitating to the spirit. However, for women, the experiences, thoughts and feelings they are allowed to own are often too little prized by our culture. One well-known study by the psychologist I. K. Broverman asked male and female participants to select from a series of adjectives those that they considered to be qualities of a healthy adult, a healthy man and a healthy woman. While the participants—regardless of sex—identified the qualities of a healthy man to be identical with a healthy adult, they did not select the same qualities for a healthy woman. For instance, healthy women were described as illogical, dependent, passive, weak and childish, while healthy adults and men were described as logical, independent, active, strong and mature. The results point out that in our culture it is difficult to be viewed as both a woman and an adult. The feminist movement has not decreased the pressures on adolescent girls, according to Pipher, because the "lip service paid to equality makes the reality of discrimination even more confusing."[3]

Girls often turn, in their confusion, to their mothers, trusting that their mothers will guide them through the acculturation process and understand their anger and frustration. Unfortunately, mothers are often baffled by their daughters' behavior. The mothers themselves may not fully have accepted both the feminine and masculine aspects of their own personalities and may bear scars or still festering wounds from their own maturation process. They may even find their daughters' behavior a challenge and threat to the tenuous balance they have achieved in their own lives. Or perhaps they have not been able to achieve any balance for themselves, and so are unable to help another.

At the same time, daughters want to reject their mothers, bitter that these older women let themselves be trapped by the very same processes which are trapping the girls, furious that the mothers are even in league with the forces which are trapping them, having taught their girls to behave in ways that are socially acceptable: Be smart, but not too smart, because the boys won't like you. Be independent, but not too independent, because you will need a husband and family. Be strong, but not too strong, because people are threatened by aggressive and ambitious women. Be honest, but don't say anything that might hurt anyone. Be beautiful, but not too beautiful, because you're just asking men to make sexual advances. Be a mother, but be a virgin, because women should be pure.

As my girls enter college and struggle to discern their futures, I find that I am torn. I want to encourage them to be intelligent, competent women, to develop and pursue their many talents and interests, but I know firsthand how difficult it is to juggle career and family and personal demands. How do I advise my daughters? When I try to tell them my story, my difficulties and challenges and how I worked them out, they say, "Don't worry, Mom. We won't be like you." Why not? Am I such a failure? But do I really want them to be like me? Isn't that why I am telling them my story, so they will be different? Their words sting.

There is no greater insult for many women than to be told they are just like their mothers. Yet Pipher, after years of working with adolescents, asserts that a girl who hates her mother hates herself. Now, loving her mother does not mean that a daughter must approve or accept all that the mother became. Nor does loving her mother mean that she must approve or accept all that the mother wants her to become. What it does mean is that the daughter understands that her mother is a woman, too, besieged by the same cultural forces, negative criticisms, confusions, doubts, fears and temptations that besiege her. Many of us—mothers and daughters alike—do feel that we died as persons in adolescence, and what is left of us is nothing of value—empty dreams and fizzled passions. But that is where we are wrong.

Listening to the Voices

We learned in Luke's healing stories that women need healing in the area of purposeful activity, in the area of being, of self-identity. The problem with being a cripple, an outcast, a slave, a poor person, a woman (all underdogs in Luke's Gospel) is that you begin to love your position of servility. It's all you know. Freedom involves too many changes, too many risks. The temptation is to remain a slave.

For women, the temptation is three-pronged. First, women often avoid speaking words of power to power. They would rather have peace at any cost than to engender conflict. However, conflict is sometimes not only unavoidable but absolutely necessary for growth to occur. We'll say more about this later.

Second, women also often adhere slavishly to tradition. They tend to be the keepers of the hearth, preserving and nurturing the family, Church and community rituals. Yet, far too often, the ritual may become more important to women than the meaning within the ritual. I once heard about a woman whose husband asked her why she always chopped off the end of the ham before she put it in the roasting pan to bake. Was she saving the piece for something else? Did the procedure help the ham's flavor? She really didn't know, she had to admit, except that her mother had always done it. So she asked her mother. It turns out that she shortened the ham because that was what her mother had always done. When Grandmother was finally asked, she explained that her roasting pan was too small for the hams then available in the market, so she cut the ham to fit the pan. The story is humorous, but it points out how we often do things simply because that is the way they have always been done.

Third, women often stifle growth for fear of the risks. Now fear itself is not an evil. Fear is actually extremely useful because it tells us when we are in the presence of danger, of evil. There is nothing shameful about fear; in fact, if we cease to be afraid, we have become numb to the evil around us. Women are often afraid for the ones they love because to love makes one vulnerable to danger, to being deeply hurt or grieved. But we cannot let fear paralyze us, drown our hope, weaken our resolve. We must learn to live with fear in courage and in love.

One frightening experience for many mothers is to let their teenagers start driving. I was not prepared for the tumult I underwent every time one of the girls backed out of the garage. Hearing sirens wailing on the highway or a news report about an automobile accident involving young people increased my panic. I wanted to drive them everywhere, but knew I had to let go. I could not control every circumstance. I had to trust my girls, the other drivers and God. I had to trust that I could live with whatever happened. How I learned to handle this fear was to quiz the girls about where they were going, how long they would be there and what routes they thought they would be taking. The girls thought I was checking up on them—which is fine—but what I was really doing was calculating just when they would be on the road. I only allowed myself to worry during that time. Of course, what eventually happened is that I got so busy with my own occupations while they were gone that I forgot to watch the clock. Suddenly they would be walking in the kitchen door—and I hadn't even worried! I have yet to lose my fear for their safety, but I have learned to accept it and to live with it.

If we are to keep from being Martha in Luke's story, we must hear the angels urging us to sit at Jesus' feet like Mary and begin the process of self-discovery. We must let God serve us. We must find out who we really are. Theologian Karl Rahner argues that to develop our personal self is also to develop our experience of God. To lose our self-identity, therefore, is to lose the experience of God.

Don't worry about selfishly abandoning God on this journey of self-discovery. Remember that in Luke's Gospel, women do not desert Jesus at the cross. They were just as afraid as the men were, but they had learned to live with that fear, not to let that fear paralyze them and keep them from acting, from witnessing, from loving. Jesus had stood up for them when they were broken; they do not desert him when he is broken and dying. The strength he gave them to be whole and complete individual daughters of God allows them to remain firm.

Remember, too, that other young Mary who said "yes" to the angel who came to her and became pregnant with possibility. Will you give birth to the woman God meant you to be?

Questions for Reflection and Discussion

- *Read about Mary's angelic visitor in Luke's Gospel (1:26-38). Have you ever thought of those inner urges to change as "angelic voices"? In what ways does the Gospel account of the angelic voice speaking to Mary ring true with your experience of the call to change in your life? Or does the account connect with your experience at all?*

- *For the next week, be attentive to how popular culture portrays women—television shows, magazine advertisements, musical lyrics. What is our youth learning about the roles of women?*

- *Describe a beautiful woman. Now define beauty. Of the women you know, how many of them are beautiful by your definition? Are you?*

- *Describe how you are beautiful to God.*

- *How has your relationship with your mother changed over the years? What do you wish your mother had said or done for you? Why do you think she wasn't able to?*

- *If you have a daughter, identify how your relationship with her has changed as she has matured. What are your hopes for her? Fears for her? What do you wish you could do for her if it were possible, if she would let you?*

- *How did you choose to express your call to conversion? Why? Keep the finished piece in a location where you will frequently see it and be reminded of the woman you are: at your computer or desk, on your bedroom nightstand or the windowsill near the kitchen sink, attached to the bathroom mirror.*

Notes

[1] Joann Wolski Conn. *Women's Spirituality: Resources for Christian Development* (Mahwah, N.J.: Paulist Press, 1986), p. 11.

[2] Mary Pipher, Ph.D. *Reviving Ophelia: Saving the Selves of Adolescent Girls* (New York: G. P. Putnam's Sons, 1994), p. 44.

[3] Pipher, p. 11.

CHAPTER FIVE

Toward a Female Spirituality

> ***Activity:*** *Again using the medium of your choice, make a representation of the demons or the "monsters" which plague you—the sins, temptations, failings you wrestle with or the negative voices and criticism you hear. Some people find it cathartic to ritually destroy these representations. Offer the demons to God in prayer, then burn or dismantle your creations.*

When my father died unexpectedly, the community's response was so wonderfully overwhelming at first that my family will never be able adequately to express our gratitude for their love and support. However, as anyone knows who has had to sit with grief, there came a certain point in the calendar—and I'm not quite sure precisely when it was—when the community expected us to be done with grieving. A very close male friend of mine said to me that I wasn't handling my dad's death like he thought I would. Well, no, I guess I wasn't. And if the truth were told, I wasn't handling it like I thought I would. At first there was a sense of loss, which is to be expected, but then came feelings that were anything but expected: I experienced a crushing sense of personal failure. Whenever I made the mistake of mentioning this, well-meaning friends would lecture me about all my accomplishments. How could I possibly feel that I was a failure? How could I possibly, indeed? Yet I did, and their words only exacerbated my condition because I was not allowed to acknowledge how I felt. I grew more and more silent and withdrawn and depressed. An avid writer and reader, I could not write for months and did not want to read, either.

I had always suspected that my father had felt failure all too keenly, having lost his business, then suffered through a series of jobs that didn't quite work out for him. He was even fired from one. Slowly I became aware that I was drawing parallels in our lives: I, too, had suffered some major career setbacks, some of them of my own choosing, others not. I began to wonder what Dad had thought of me, if he had seen me as a failure, too. I began to wonder what he thought of himself.

Eventually I was able to write about my father. Doing so allowed me to own my experiences and feelings. I reevaluated my definition of success. And I reclaimed my past as mine, not as a life lived under his approving or disapproving gaze—nor anyone else's, for that matter.

Women and Relationships

Although my grief process confounded my friends, my family and even myself, it was, I later discovered, not really that unusual. Carol Gilligan, a psychologist who has studied female life development, has discovered that often women experience the disruption of a relationship as not only a loss of the relationship, but also as a loss of self. Children leaving home for college, a divorce or the death of a family member may affect women in ways that baffle others and, perhaps, even baffle themselves. I have known women who slid into serious bouts of depression requiring medical intervention after their youngest child left home while their husbands watched helplessly. My own situation was compounded by the fact that my eldest child had entered college only a few months before Dad died.

It is not that relationships are more important for women than for men. It is not that women grieve more than men do. I have witnessed in my own small community the devastating loss men feel after the death of a child or a spouse, and a woman friend told me in genuine awe that her husband cries after each phone call they receive from their college daughter. I am also not surprised—although greatly saddened—when an elderly neighbor abandons the struggle for life after his wife of fifty years dies, dying himself soon afterwards. Rather it is that women define their very identity in a context of relationship, judging their worth by a standard of responsibility and care—at least this was so for every woman interviewed in Gilligan's study.

In the traditional idea of human development, women, triggered by the loss of relationships at midlife because their children are grown or they have experienced family deaths, return to the unfinished business of adolescence, the business of separation from family and growth into autonomy. That is, of course, the male model, which has always suggested that women never complete their separation from parents and which has always depicted women as mired in relationships. (I remember my mother halfheartedly complaining after a parent-teacher conference for me that she had always been known as "someone else's": She used to be introduced as her parents' daughter, then her husband's wife and now, when she finally thought she could be the possessor and not the possessed, she was known as her children's mother. It just didn't seem fair, she laughed.) But is the male model the ideal model for all humans?

Gilligan's research would suggest otherwise. For a male, leaving childhood means that he renounces parental relationships, especially his relationship with his mother, in order to achieve autonomy, the certainty of his own beliefs and his freedom of self-expression. The search for autonomy often wins for a man respect, approval and even relationships. However, highly successful men have very few attachments. One has only to read the lives of Martin Luther or Mahatma Gandhi for examples. In fact, men will often see relationships as qualifying their identity rather than helping them realize it. Men define their identity through achievements, accomplishments.

However, the development for women is often much different. Rather than separation, women's lives are usually characterized by the ongoing process of attachment, a process that creates and sustains the community. Rather than a search for more autonomy and freedom of self-expression, women often relinquish these qualities in order to preserve relationships or to protect others. Autonomy frequently becomes a dangerous word for women. Such acts of relinquishment often lead women to see themselves as powerless and helpless, constantly compromised. Yet at other times they will feel power and magnanimity precisely from the self-sacrifice. Rather than seeing relationships as jeopardizing their identity, women see professional achievements and accomplishments as jeopardizing their relationships, thus also jeopardizing their identity.

Spiritual Development Patterns

It would seem logical, therefore, that since the development patterns are different for women and men, their spiritual development patterns will be different also. That is just what Gilligan discovered. For a man, the path of adult spiritual development will lead him from autonomy to intimacy, bringing to an end his isolation and indifference toward others, and leading him toward adult love. For a woman, the opposite is true. At some point she must realize that she, too, should be included in the group of people she cares for and nurtures, that she, too, is a member of the group it is moral not to hurt. Whereas the transformative spiritual experience for men is intimacy; for a woman, it is choice—the choice to be true to herself as well as true to the people she loves.

The dilemma, therefore, is really the same for both sexes: the conflict between personal integrity and the care for others. Male development emphasizes the absolute value of personal integrity, giving rise to an ethic of justice, an ethic embedded in rights, fairness, equality and reciprocity, truth and respect. Female development emphasizes the absolute value of care, giving rise to an ethic of responsibility, embedded in compassion, generosity and a desire not to hurt others. For spiritual growth to occur, the individual must move away from the absolute that has up to then defined him or her and move toward the direction of the other qualities. The result will be both a fuller sense of self and fuller relationships. Rather than seeing the "self" as something that is against another, threatened and opposed by another, the more mature spiritual vision is that the true self is not totally separated from the other, but grows with the other alternately through identification and differentiation into a mutually enhancing relationship. What had once been thought to be opposites can now be held together in a constantly evolving synthesis: the self and the other, matter and spirit, God and human, love and power, being and doing, private and public, compassion and self-affirmation.

The point is that men's and women's spiritual paths are often very different, yet far too often women have tried to follow the male model, frequently to their detriment. Trying to move from the personal integrity perspective to the care perspective caused me much anguish since I had not yet defined my own personal integrity. I should have been moving in the opposite direction. For twenty years I struggled against what I thought was a selfish desire to become a writer in favor of teaching, which seemed to me the better way to serve God. What else could I add to the world of ideas, I asked myself. How will the world be better with one more book in it? Isn't it escapism to live in my imagination for hours upon hours?

Finally I realized that writing ultimately has nothing to do with publication and potential readers. Writing is a solitary pilgrimage into the center of my being. What I most feared during those twenty years was that I would not like what I would find there at my center, or worse yet, I would find only emptiness there. And, too, I realized that my teaching was actually rooted in the ego, in the need for my students and colleagues to assure me that I did have something to offer, that I was a worthwhile and good person. I had to learn to open myself, let go and trust the writing process to take me where I was supposed to go. I quit my job and gave myself one experimental year as a full-time writer. Facing the blank page every day was more difficult than facing a room full of students, because I couldn't hide behind my notes and textbooks and grade book; for the first time I had to squarely face my own thoughts and ideas. What I always thought of as a selfish dream has proven to be the most self-denying thing I have ever done.

Paradoxically, beginning this solitary pilgrimage on paper has made me more open and accepting of others. I don't see my students, now that I've returned to teaching, as vessels that have to be filled with knowledge and experience, but as fellow sojourners on the way to truth. I am more relaxed and happy around my friends and family now and recognize the great gifts they are to me. I have touched others with my written words, inspiring them to write and to read and to begin their own journeys to discover self. (By eschewing publication for a time, I have been granted a receptive audience, although not the audience I would have guessed.) My husband said the enthusiastic, dream-filled and hopeful girl he married was back. I thought she was lost. She hadn't been lost, merely imprisoned by years of neglect. What if she had died in her prison? What would have been left of me? What would I have been able to offer others then?

My journey is my journey, of course. Each woman will have to find her own way. Sometimes that way may seem to conflict with everything she has been taught about the spiritual journey, but she must remember that often what she was taught was the male model that has eclipsed female experiences and female models of spirituality. Let's reexamine one model of female spirituality: the model of Mary, Jesus' mother.

Mary

There are two ways of speaking of Mary's holiness, both of them deriving from Luke's presentation of her. The traditional way is to see Mary as the sinless virgin and mother, a model of humility and selfless devotion. However, some feminist scholars caution that we must be careful in our devotion not to idealize her until she becomes a kind of "goddess." Luke certainly does not present her this way. Rather, Luke presents Mary as the first disciple. Because we are called to be disciples, we likewise are all to "give birth" to Christ, to make Christ apparent to the world. We are all graced in this mission. And we all carry out the mission through graced human endeavor. To say otherwise precludes us from imitating Mary.

Mary herself in Luke's Gospel characterizes herself as a slave (1:38; new translations upgrade the language from bond slave or handmaiden to servant). She, therefore, becomes a model of submissiveness, dependence and helplessness. As a result, Mary seems passive to many readers of Luke's Gospel, submitting to God, husband, son, political authorities and the early Church leaders.

Yet the Magnificat Mary sings is not the song of a passive victim (1:46-55). She praises God at the same time that she realizes her own worth. She will now be called blessed by ages to come, not, according to her prayer, because she has virginally conceived but because she has remained faithful, recognized the Messianic message of the angel and will witness the rehabilitation of Israel as God promised to all who remain faithful to the Law. Julia Esquivel, a Guatemalan teacher, poet and human rights advocate, sees her as the model of prophetic freedom:

> *Mary, the young peasant from Nazareth, is a paradigm for all women who have faith and hope for a new society in which human life is the most sacred value. Engaged to an artisan, Mary was preparing herself for a married life. But the intervention of the God of the poor superseded that dream and project for something larger, a plan for her own people and for all of humanity.*[1]

So the second way to talk about Mary's holiness is as a woman on the universal quest for liberation and wholeness. When she calls herself a slave, she is not passively acquiescing to the will of another (even though that other is God), but actively accepting God, linking her will with God's will. When she calls herself a slave, she is actually using for herself the honorable Jewish title of "slave of God"—a title applied to Abraham, Isaac, Joshua, Moses, David and the prophets. When we consider all the other allusions to biblical themes Luke has woven into this first chapter of his Gospel, we begin to see that Luke's description of Mary is far more complicated than that of a passive virgin. Elizabeth and Zachariah recall another aged and childless couple, Sarah and Abraham, and God's power to make fertile what is not. We hear echoes of Samson's birth to Manoa, which was also announced by an angel, and Samuel's birth to Hannah. The angel who visits Mary is Gabriel, the angel who appeared to Daniel in the Old Testament, announcing the beginning of the end times. The spirit overshadowing Mary reminds us of God's presence above the Ark in Exodus. God dwells with his people, first in the form of fire and smoke; now in the form of a man, Jesus. The child leaping in Elizabeth's womb at Mary's greeting recalls Esau and Jacob leaping in Rebekah's womb. Are John and Jesus the new Esau and Jacob where the older (i.e., the Law, the Covenant) serves the younger (the Christ, the fulfillment and realization of the Covenant)? Joseph and Mary's journey to Bethlehem sounds very much like the journey Jacob made with his pregnant wife Rachel to his homeland, Bethlehem, where Rachel gave birth to Benjamin. Joseph and

Mary's losing Jesus as a child reminds us of how Jacob lost Joseph. And like Jacob, Mary pondered, treasured everything in her heart.

These allusions suggest that Mary's life should be seen within the context of God's Messianic promises to all of the chosen people. Mary is the New Israel, willingly and joyfully accepting both God's promises and the world's persecution in order to realize the Kingdom that has now broken through with the birth of its Messiah. She is anything but passive. As such, her life challenges women to their own spiritual acceptance of God's promises and the world's persecution.

A better way to look at spiritual development, then, is not to reject one model in favor of another, but to see that the male and female models are mutually enhancing, having much to teach each other. Mary represents the response of the perfect disciple in two ways. She represents the absolute value of care, exhibiting obedient trust, self-sacrifice and an intimacy with God that was unparalleled. She also represents the absolute value of personal integrity, believing in her own worth despite what the voices of the world around her proclaimed: You are poor; you are a woman, an unwed mother, lowly. She knew that in God's eyes she was much more. She was beautiful, mighty, grand. She was blessed.

Questions for Reflection and Discussion

- *Describe your devotion to Mary. What factors shaped your attitude toward her? Has your attitude changed over the years? Why, do you think?*
- *Who have been your models of the spiritual life? What about these models attracted you to them? How would you characterize their spiritual lives?*
- *Has it been true in your experience that women often find professional responsibilities and accomplishments threatening not only to important relationships in their lives, but*

to their own sense of identity?

- *Describe your feelings and reactions to a lost relationship: a broken friendship, divorce, the "empty nest" stage when the children left home or the death of a loved one.*
- *If you were to include yourself in the group of loved ones you care for, what would you do in order to nurture yourself?*

Note

[1] Kathleen Fischer. *Women at the Well: Feminist Perspectives on Spiritual Direction* (New York: Paulist Press, 1988), p. 36.

PART THREE

The Hand That Rocks the Cradle

Chapter Six

Sell All You Have

Activity: *Compare the Beatitudes of Matthew (5:1-11) with those of Luke (6:20-26). What differences do you note? What would you say is the emphasis of Matthew's version? Of Luke's version? Given what we have said so far about the central message of Luke's Gospel, why do you think he chose the wording that he did? Which version speaks more powerfully to you? Why?*

Let's begin with a brief case study. Political analysts who looked at the voting patterns of men and women in the 1996 United States presidential election determined that American women were responsible for Bill Clinton's reelection. While the majority of men voted for his opponent, the majority of women voted for Clinton, presumably because his social programs—health care reform, education packages, welfare expenditures, child-care programs and so on—enticed them. Although Clinton's second term in office was marked by scandal, perjury and eventual impeachment, the case study corroborates two striking trends in women's involvement in the political sphere:

1. *Women have come into political power*—both as individual political candidates and as a powerful block of voters. In the past, analysts decried the fact that women tended to vote the same as the men in their households, in actuality, therefore, merely doubling their husbands' votes—if they voted at all. Until the mid-1900's, women in North America and Europe were less interested than men in political issues and were less likely to vote. Now, it would seem, we are beginning to use our newfound voices. Since 1980, the number of women voters has increased dramatically, as well as the number of women candidates. In the United States, female voters now outnumber their male counterparts, making up fifty-four percent of the presidential electorate. We women are learning that we can influence our leaders in ways other than simply rearing them when they are young, as the adage reminded us: The hand that rocks the cradle rules the world. A question for us now is how are we, as Christians, to best use that power?

2. *Women tend to focus on the candidates' social programs, not their foreign or military policies.* Recent exit polls and surveys reveal that women are more likely than men to support government programs that guarantee health care, jobs and annual income, provide wage and price controls and equalize wealth, protect the environment and reduce violent crime. They are also more likely than men to oppose capital punishment, deregulation of handguns and military and defense spending. Do these issues indicate that women are more compassionate and moral (as some would argue) or that they seek greater security and control over their lives? Should social programs be the proper focus for us?

The Scriptures cannot, of course, directly answer these questions for us, but they can provide a context within which we can begin to search for our own answers.

We saw earlier that, according to Luke, the appropriate

response to God's bountiful mercy is a revolution of mind and heart. Such a revolution is bound to cause changes in our behavior toward others. We will want to share God's merciful love with others. That is, in fact, the basis of Luke's ethic: Be good, love one another, give alms, take up the cross daily, pray always. But what about the larger social issues of justice and poverty and oppression? Does Luke address those?

The Poor in Luke

Luke has often been called the evangelist of the poor. However, these poor he writes about in his Gospel are not so easy to accept. Not only do they include outcasts, sinners and women with bad reputations, but also individuals who challenge our entire way of life. We can tolerate the first group if they repent and clean up, but there is no tolerating the second, for they demand that we change and change radically. We are the ones, these poor assert, who need to clean up and repent.

Take, for instance, the shepherds who were the first to worship the infant Jesus (2:8-20). Matthew describes the first worshippers as Magi: intelligent and worldly-wise men who use their knowledge of astronomy to discover the newborn king in Judea. But Luke focuses instead upon the lowly, not the worldly-wise. Now Luke's shepherds are not the pastoral figures so often represented in nativity scenes. Rather they were social deviants: one of the more violence-prone groups in rural areas during Jesus' time because they were blatantly careless of where their flocks grazed. As a result, they were often embroiled in bloody struggles with the villagers who had succumbed to rage at seeing their crops devoured by the woolly grazers. Not exactly the peaceful, nature-loving group we had imagined!

Or examine once again Mary's Magnificat (1:46-55) in which she praises God for upsetting the balance of power: toppling the rich and powerful so that the poor and weak may replace them. Or what about the parable of the feast (14:15-

24) where the privileged are rejected in favor of the maimed, the outcast and the poor? This parable is particularly powerful when we recall that Leviticus forbids the maimed and blemished from offering oblations to God, or from even approaching God's altar (Leviticus 21:16-23). Jesus has not simply extended table fellowship to everyone, but has "turned the tables" on those who had been originally invited: They are no longer welcome. Or we could look at how Luke's beatitudes (6:20-26) differ from Matthew's (5:1-11). Matthew emphasizes religious and spiritual values of those who are in the kingdom: They are poor in spirit; they hunger and thirst for righteousness. Luke, on the other hand, addresses real economic and social conditions of humanity: blessed are the poor; blessed are the hungry. Woe, however, to the rich for they have already had their consolation. The kingdom will radically reduce them to poverty, and they will endure hunger and grief.

Jesus' teachings, which in all the Gospels are highly critical of the status quo, encouraged some of his disciples to demand political solutions to oppression. Because many of the poor had lost their lands to more powerful, greedy and unscrupulous creditors, these disciples desired the forgiveness of debt and land redistribution. Therefore, the early Jesus movement had strong overtones of rural unrest and protest.

The Rich in Luke

Luke tries to temper this more radical movement within the Christian community, which could lead to violence between the haves and have-nots, while at the same time calling the rich to compassion and conversion. For, you see, Luke is not really the evangelist of the poor, but of the rich, of those who want the status quo. Note that he addresses his Gospel to his most excellent patron Theophilus (1:1-4). Theophilus may be a real person or he may just be a literary convention, but either way, it would seem that Luke's audience is not the

Jewish poor, but the economically comfortable gentiles in Antioch, Syria, the probable location of Luke's community.

Antioch was the next largest city to Rome in the Empire, and her citizens were in awe of Rome's power and orderly control of so many disparate peoples. The citizens of Antioch were concerned with maintaining a stable society, which included, to them, the very real economic necessity of slavery. (You'll recall that Paul, another evangelist to the gentiles, does not advocate the abolition of slavery, but encourages all to remain in their current stations in life until Jesus comes again. See his first letter to the Corinthians, 7:17-24.) These gentiles in Luke's audience would also have seen the humility of Jesus and of Mary as servility rather than something to be admired and imitated. Here was a man who died the death of a rebellious slave. They would have found such a person difficult to accept. But Luke shows Jesus to be a true hero. He suffers death, that is true, but not degradation, and it is a death freely chosen. Jesus remains always in control, much like Prometheus and Achilles—heroes Luke's audience would admire. During his arrest, trial, torture and death, Jesus continues directly and indirectly his "heroic"—or saving—work, healing the slave's ear, consoling the women on the way, forgiving the sinner on the cross. Yet Luke's audience still preferred nobility and freedom, which were the conditions of their privileged status as free Roman citizens.

So, in many ways, they sound a lot like us. We, too, are enamored with power and order and maintaining the status quo. We, too, are impressed with the nobility of rank and aristocracy—whether an aristocracy based on birth or acquired wealth. Luke had quite a challenge in making the Christian message understandable to his urban gentile audience, just as many first-world Christians today find Luke's Gospel a challenge to understand. Luke's Magnificat and his Sermon on the Plain appear, if not revolutionary, preposterous. In fact, Frederick W. Danker, in his *Luke*, argues that the ethical guidelines Luke presents are not only impractical, but suicidal. As the story of Jesus' conversation with the rich man seems to illustrate, the only proper use of wealth is to get rid of it (18:18-30).

Now all the Gospels portray Jesus in opposition to wealth. But Luke's Gospel expands this theme in greater detail. Whereas in both Mark and Matthew, Jesus tells the rich man to sell his possessions and give to the poor (Mark 10:21 and Matthew 19:21), in Luke, Jesus tells him to sell *all* that he has (18:22). When the first disciples are called, Mark and Matthew tell us that they left father and boat (that is, their occupations or livelihood) to follow Jesus (Mark 1:20 and Matthew 4:22). But Luke tells us that they left *all* (5:11). In Matthew's Gospel, when Jesus teaches about perseverance in prayer, he assures the believer that the Father will give good things to those who ask (7:11). In Luke, Jesus says that the Father does not give things to those who ask, but gives the Holy Spirit (11:13). Matthew writes, "Do not store up for yourselves treasures on earth, where moth and rust consume and where thieves break in and steal; but store up for yourselves treasures in heaven, where neither moth nor rust consumes and where thieves do not break in and steal. For where your treasure is, there your heart will be also" (6:19-22 *NRSV).* Luke changes the passage when he writes, "Sell your possessions, and give alms. Make purses for yourselves that do not wear out, an unfailing treasure in heaven, where no thief comes near and no moth destroys. For where your treasure is, there your heart will be also" (12:33-34 *NRSV).*

We often console ourselves that the Gospels do not really condemn wealth itself, but rather condemn us when we concentrate too greatly upon the acquisition of wealth at the expense of our own spiritual lives or others' physical needs. Yet although the other Gospels, especially the spirituality behind Matthew's beatitudes, may tell us that there is a place for wealthy individuals in Christianity as long as they maintain a spirit of detachment toward their possessions, Luke is not so accommodating. Luke seems to be attacking wealth itself.

Only in Luke do we find the story of the landowner who, because of a bumper crop, reinvests his capital in order to expand his grain storage facilities (12:15-21). By any worldly standards, the man is making a sound business decision, not necessarily a greedy one, but Jesus brands him as a blasphemous fool who stored up earthly riches instead of spiritual ones. And only in Luke do we have the parable of Lazarus and the Rich Man (16:19-31). A careful reading of the parable reveals that the rich man did not live a dissolute life. No, the story simply tells us that he enjoyed his wealth. Later, when he cries out from Hades for relief, Abraham tells him, "My child, remember that you were well off in your lifetime, while Lazarus was in misery. Now he has found consolation here, but you have found torment" (16:25).

In Acts, Luke portrays the early Church as ideally following Jesus' orders about wealth in their communal living. Many members sold what they had and gave the proceeds to the community to be distributed as needed (2:43-47 and 4:32-37). One husband and wife who attempted to deceive the community and God by keeping back some of the proceeds for themselves were dealt with severely by God (5:1-11). Not only would the rich find this style of communal living challenging, but also the peasants who wanted their lands back. They would feel they had merely exchanged one tyrannical landlord for another.

Why are the rich condemned? Before we can answer this, we must first examine what wealth represents. What we own often becomes an extension of ourselves—our homes, businesses, automobiles, clothing. What we buy reflects both our needs and our desires. So our possessions can become symbols of ourselves—of our values, longings, occupations and preoccupations. Possessions can symbolically express our identity. Luke shows that how an individual disposes of his possessions reveals whether his identity is as one of God's children or one of the world's citizens. An individual's use of wealth after meeting Jesus reveals whether he accepts or rejects the Word. So, although at first reading Luke seems to be attacking wealth, he is really attacking a certain kind of disposition, a disposition that presents a closed fist to God rather than an open hand.

We have so far focused on the more radical claims Jesus makes on a disciple, but Luke actually shows various approaches to using wealth. Some disciples, such as the Good Samaritan, give alms, some share all goods in common within the Christian community and some do renounce all. Remember that the Christian community was persecuted by both Jews and gentiles, and is sometimes still persecuted today. Becoming a Christian just may mean the complete renunciation of all we have, even our lives. Are we willing to abandon ourselves to God?

So one answer to why the rich are condemned is that they consider themselves self-sufficient and not in need of God. Luke is not praising poverty itself, for we all know that abject poverty can grind the spirit into despair or even destroy the spirit, resulting in crimes of brutality and desperation. Rather, the poor are blessed because, lacking physical comforts, they need and depend entirely upon God. The poor are those who are unable to demand justice for themselves; therefore they trust in God's justice. The poor are the barren Elizabeth, the widow who lost her son, the ostracized disabled—all whose situations are impossible to rectify. Their only hope is God.

But the rich are condemned for another reason as well. How an individual disposes of possessions also reveals how he relates to others, especially the play of power between persons. The Greco-Roman culture did not practice almsgiving unless there was some expectation of a return, a kind of I.O.U. system. The benefactor would expect something for his charity: a similar favor later if the needy person was a friend and equal; privileges or titles if his superior; statues, inscriptions or obedient service if the needy person was below his rank and station. Such an attitude does not necessarily make one calculating and cruel, but it does tend to make one insensitive to the needs of those outside one's circle of influence. That is, I believe, the case of the rich man and Lazarus. Lazarus is so removed from the rich man's network of relationships that he can make no demand upon the rich man's charity.

Yet the parable reveals that Christians should minister to the powerless, not only as fulfillment of the covenant (for Moses and the prophets called for the powerful to care for the powerless), but as a sign of the unity—in both body and heart—among all God's people. Therefore, the rich are condemned because they let their wealth weave a veil of security and complacency around them, separating them from and blinding them to the suffering of others.

Yet there is a third reason the rich are condemned. The widow who drops two small coins into the temple treasury is also poor (21:1-4). Jesus praises her because she gives from her need, rather than giving from abundance as the wealthy do (21:1-4), but he also is criticizing the temple authorities that have maintained the temple surroundings and their comfortable lifestyles at the expense of just such as these widows. In a world that believed that all goods were limited and finite, for someone to gain meant that someone else had to lose. Those who were rich had the power to take from those who were poor and lacked the power to defend what they did have. Remember that Luke's audience wanted stability. Just how is the status quo maintained, Luke seems to be asking. Is it due to the schemes and projects of the wealthy, or the sweat and blood of the poor?

Such a message would not be willingly embraced by Luke's audience. Becoming a Christian provided a social haven for the poor but social disaster for the rich. They cannot hang on to their old way of life in this community. How can Luke reach this audience that is wondering whether possessions and elitism prevent the rich and the powerful from being genuine Christians?

His solution is to present Jesus as a great Roman benefactor. You'll recall that Luke's audience is in awe of Rome's power and orderly control of her many subjects. So Luke describes Jesus as possessing just these qualities. He is a kingly lord who did good in word and deed, who brought peace and prosperity and who was politically original.

Luke's Jesus is a powerful orator and performer of mighty deeds. At the age of twelve, he astounds the elders with his knowledge. He breaks taboos without fear of consequences. He grants pardon for sins. He performs many miracles, especially at the start of his ministry. Several of these are recorded only in Luke: the miraculous catch of fish that prompts the first disciples to follow him (5:1-11; compare to Matthew 4:18-22 or Mark 1:16-20 where no miracle is performed), the raising of the widow's son (7:11-16), the expulsion of evil spirits in the women who accompanied him (8:1-2), the crippled woman (13:10-17), the man with dropsy (14:1-6) and the ten lepers (17:12-19). And, of course, the greatest deed of all is God's resurrection of Jesus. Later, on the road to Emmaus, his interpretation of Moses and the prophets to Cleopas and his companion (perhaps Cleopas's wife) causes their hearts to burn within them (24:13-35). Jesus' life, mission and death bring salvation to the world.

Jesus also brings peace and sustenance to his people. "Peace be with you," the resurrected Jesus says to his frightened disciples (24:36). His mission is characterized by feeding others. Every chapter in Luke includes food: Jesus is often found at table, sharing a meal; he feeds the multitudes; he offers his own life as food for others in the bread and wine at the Last Supper. He is accused of being a glutton and drunkard (7:34) who breaks religious and social taboos by breaking bread with sinners. For Judaism, to share the broken bread was also to share the blessing that the host spoke over the unbroken bread. Eating, therefore, becomes for Luke an acted parable. Food is life; sharing food is sharing life. Jesus' table fellowship signifies a deeper hospitality than merely entertaining invited guests. Rather it signifies that, through Jesus' word and life, God feeds all of hungry creation. Jesus shuns a lifestyle of being waited upon in order to become God's "table servant," and he demands the same of his disciples.

Finally, Jesus is the great Roman benefactor through his truly original political ideology. Jesus teaches that the truly great benefactors find greatness by being the least—not the most powerful. Such a position puts him in stark contrast with the world, and Luke portrays the devil as Jesus' political adversary. In the temptation scene, Luke clearly draws lines of conflict from the start, and the devil's temptation is phrased in the language of political power:

> *Then the devil led him up and showed him in an instant all the kingdoms of the world. And the devil said to him, "To you I will give their glory and all this authority; for it has been given over to me, and I give it to anyone I please. If you, then, will worship me, it will all be yours."* (4:5-7, NRSV)

You misunderstand how things work, the devil is saying. Be practical. This is how it is done in the world. I have friends in high places. Therefore, if you want to get things done, you're going to have to play the game, my game. And the game is all about power and cash. Don't ever forget that. Later Judas will betray you (22:3) for just this reason—because you did not play the game.

Therefore, to be a disciple of Jesus means that we must denounce the "game" as well. We must renounce all worldly criteria of success: financial reward, social status, accolades and promotions. Instead we must define success by whether or not we live a life of righteousness and justice.

When Jesus dies, the Roman centurion who witnessed the crucifixion proclaims that certainly this must have been an innocent man, just and righteous (23:47). This is not what the centurion says in Matthew or Mark. There he proclaims Jesus as the Son of God (Matthew 27:54; Mark 15:39). Luke in this passage underscores the value his audience prized most in a great man: not a divine birthright, but excellence of character.

And just what was this excellence of character? What did the centurion see at Jesus' death? For one thing, there was Jesus' integrity throughout all the temptations to save himself during the arrest, trial and crucifixion. There was Jesus' prayer of forgiveness for his oppressors, and his ministry to the criminal dying alongside him. There was the dark that shrouded Jesus' death. There was the revelation of Jesus as God's temple, available to all, in contrast to the Jerusalem temple that veiled God's presence. At Jesus' death, the temple curtain was torn in two. There was the absolute trust Jesus placed in his Father. Ultimately, there was God's very presence with Jesus—and through Jesus with all of creation—in and through death.

Yes, Jesus' life, mission and death serve as a powerful criticism of the status quo. Yet he never advocates specific social or political policies. In fact, Luke—the great advocate to the rich for the poor—seems to temper the more radical claims Jesus makes in Mark and Matthew. For example, you will not find anywhere in Luke the statement that the meek will inherit the earth. He also balances Mary's Magnificat, which calls for social reversal, with the Sermon on the Plain, which decries all wealth. I suspect that Luke was well aware of the dangers of reversing the balance of power. His church in Acts, although communal, is no communistic system accomplished through the united effort of the underclasses to overthrow the powerful. To simply reverse the balance of power is not the answer, for the poor, in anger over past injustices, may become worse tyrants and oppressors.

But more importantly, Luke understood what true liberty, true freedom means.

True Freedom

According to philosopher Mortimer Adler, freedom can be defined in four different ways. We in the United States tend to define freedom as, first of all, political liberty or the right of citizens to self-govern. But we also define freedom as the absence of external constraints to our ability to choose as we please and to act upon those choices. Jesus makes us aware of two other definitions that are less concerned with one's circumstances—whether one lives in a tyrannical or democratic nation, whether one's actions are bound or unbound—and more concerned with one's inner life. Therefore, a third definition of freedom is the faculty or power we possess which enables us to choose good and to do good. And fourth, freedom is self-determination, what we, as Christians, would call free will.

The problem with focusing exclusively on the first two definitions of freedom, as many of us are wont to do, is that we bind our liberty too tightly to external factors, feeling we are not free unless we have escaped despotism, poverty, illiteracy, unemployment, discrimination, disease, abuse, imprisonment, torture or whatever force "out there" is causing us to suffer and preventing us from achieving all we wish to achieve. Biographies of great people reveal that they became great often because of external challenges in their lives. Contentment breeds complacency. True liberty, therefore, is inner freedom, not outer freedom.

And the way to achieve inner freedom? Jesus constantly reminds us that seeking the path that will allow us to be rid of suffering is not the way. He also reminds us that trying to define ourselves and our freedom by our accomplishments and achievements only results in our being lost. Rather Jesus teaches that the way to freedom is through the grace of God, through empowerment by the Spirit and our own power of self-determination and our capacity to do good, regardless of the circumstances in which we find ourselves. Because of sin, it is a way that we cannot travel alone without the Spirit to guide and sustain us. The way to freedom, in fact, requires that we go *through* suffering and failure. We can never achieve true freedom if we focus solely on the alleviation of political or social conditions that limit people. Rather we must focus on the commonality of the human experience, and that experience is that we are a limited, finite creation of God subject to the pains and the suffering that result from being limited and finite. That is why Luke does not envision a world where the poor are made rich. Rather he describes a kingdom where the rich embrace the suffering of the poor in solidarity. Henri Nouwen, in *The Inner Voice of Love,* writes of this futile goal we have to name and eliminate our suffering:

> *Your pain, deep as it is, is connected with specific circumstances. You do not suffer in the abstract. You suffer because someone hurts you at a specific time and in a specific place. Your feelings of rejection, abandonment, and uselessness are rooted in the most concrete events. In this way all suffering is unique. This is eminently true of the suffering of Jesus. His disciples left him, Pilate condemned him, Roman soldiers tortured and crucified him.*
>
> *Still, as long as you keep pointing to the specifics, you will miss the full meaning of your pain. You will deceive yourself into believing that if the people, circumstances, and events had been different, your pain would not exist. This might be partly true, but the deeper truth is that the situation which brought about your pain was simply the form in which you came in touch with the human condition of suffering. Your pain is the concrete way in which you participate in the pain of humanity.*
>
> *Paradoxically, therefore, healing means moving from your pain to* the *pain. When you keep focusing on the specific circumstances of your pain, you easily become angry, resentful, and even vindictive. You are inclined to do something about the externals of your pain in order to relieve it; this explains why you often seek revenge. But real healing comes from realizing that your own particular pain is a share in humanity's pain. That realization allows you to forgive your enemies and enter into a truly compassionate life. That is the way of Jesus, who prayed on the cross: "Father forgive them; they do not know what they are doing" (Luke 23:34). Jesus' suffering, concrete as it was, was the suffering of all humanity. His* pain *was* the *pain.*

> *Every time you can shift your attention away from the external situation that caused your pain and focus on the pain of humanity in which you participate, your suffering becomes easier to bear. It becomes a "light burden" and an "easy yoke" (Matthew 11:30). Once you discover that you are called to live in solidarity with the hungry, the homeless, the prisoners, the refugees, the sick, and the dying, your very personal pain begins to be converted into* the pain and *you find new strength to live it. Herein lies the hope of all Christians.*[1]

Herein lies the way to freedom. We must find the voice to speak the words of our common pain, our common suffering, our common humanity. We must find the voice to speak of God who joined us in our humanity, our suffering, our pain.

We discussed at the beginning of our study together that we must avoid becoming fussy legalists like Martha, earning Jesus' rebuke for rushing into do-goodism instead of accomplishing real good. Often this results when we are too focused on solving the "problems" of another person's circumstance rather than truly identifying with the person and understanding his or her unique situation. Jesus' life presents us with two practices that will guide us in the right way: living in solidarity with all of humanity and practicing compassion. Let us turn toward those practices, each in turn, and examine what they can mean for women.

Questions for Reflection and Discussion

- *How important is money to you? What role does it play in your decisions about how you will spend your time, how you organize your family life, how you evaluate the job you have, how you determine the worth of everything around you?*
- *Consider all your material possessions. Which ones could you give up with ease? Which ones would cause you great anguish to lose? Are there any ways in which it could be*

said that your possessions own you rather than the other way around?

- *What were your parents' attitudes toward money?*
- *What are you teaching your children and other youngsters about money? Consider both your words and your actions.*
- *Many find Jesus' condemnation of the wealthy in Luke unsettling. What is your reaction? Which of his sayings do you find most challenging?*
- *Would you be willing to sell all you have and give the proceeds to the Church, as did some of the early Christians? Why or why not? What barriers stand in your way? What do you think the Christian attitude should be toward wealth?*
- *Perhaps your wealth is not in monetary riches, but resides in a particular gift you possess: a beautiful voice, an artistic or poetic vision, writing skills, organizational abilities, leadership skills, teaching or healing gifts. Are there any ways in which these abilities could have become impediments rather than aids to your spiritual growth? How have you used them to build community? What do Jesus' words "sell all and give to the poor" mean in the context of these possessions?*
- *How do you define success? In what ways do you rely on the world's standards to define whether or not you are successful?*
- *How do you define freedom? Identify those times in your life when you have felt free.*

Note

[1] Henri J. M. Nouwen. *The Inner Voice of Love: A Journey Through Anguish to Freedom* (New York: Doubleday, 1996), pp. 103-104.

CHAPTER SEVEN

Finding Her Voice

Activity: *After reading the parable of the corrupt judge (18:1-8), imagine yourself as the widow in the story. Why would you need to go before the judge? (Don't hesitate to answer this from your own personal experiences of injustice. You need not role-play as a first-century woman; you may be yourself.) Who would be your opponent and what is your case? Who would the judge be? How would you have firmed your resolve to speak to him? How would you have prepared yourself? Picture the scene: You are standing before him and any other people present. Have you brought someone with you for support? Imagine what you would say and do, how you would feel. Are you nervous, confident, unsure, angry, meek, resigned or hopeful? Now argue your case. What are your feelings when he refuses you? What keeps you from giving up your suit? How do your friends and neighbors respond to your repeated, and seemingly futile, efforts to attain justice through the official system?*

One of the most important and pervasive consequences of sin is alienation. The Book of Genesis makes this all too painfully clear. After Adam and Eve turned from God to the world in order to satisfy their spiritual hunger, the world's food became an insidious cancer that slowly crept into the very marrow and sinews of creation. What is so appalling about cancer is that the enemy is within: The body secretly harbors the viral intruder, nourishing it, sheltering it, until it betrays and finally kills its host. And so it is with sin. Immediately after Adam and Eve eat the fruit of the tree of the knowledge of good and evil, the cancer of alienation begins to make itself apparent. They become alienated from their very selves. They are no longer at ease with their bodies, discovering with horror that they are naked. They are unable to accept themselves as they are, as responsible agents who failed. Instead they blame each other, the serpent, anyone but who was ultimately responsible: themselves.

Then they become alienated from God, hiding from God's presence, afraid to meet God. They become alienated from nature. Their bodies are no longer under their control, but under the control of pain and death. Whereas nature once provided for all their needs in abundance, now in order to eke out a meager existence, they must labor and sweat, bleed and toil. Humans become alienated from other humans. Cain kills Abel. Murders multiply as human ferocity and arrogance increase. Sexual intimacy is perverted. By the time of the flood, humans have become totally alienated from each other, so that their very thoughts and actions are evil. By the time of the Tower of Babel, they cannot even communicate with one another.

Jesus reverses this trend. In Luke, Jesus—not the fruit offered by the devil—is God's food for hungry creation. Through his eucharistic meal of bread and wine, through his word and deed, Luke shows God, through Jesus, becoming one with us, one of us. By partaking of the bread and wine and word and deed, we become one with God, of God. And by unity with God, we become one with all of creation. We join our brothers and sisters at the great banquet. The reversal of sin, the ultimate fulfillment of God's plan, the glorious way of the kingdom, is communion, solidarity.

No wonder Jesus rebukes Martha! How foolish not to see that Jesus is her food, that he has come to nourish and sustain her—not the other way around. And note that by thinking she could serve him, she ultimately alienates herself from her sister, from the rest of the company, from Jesus' life-giving presence, and even from herself as she grumbles and complains.

To reverse this trend of alienation and to join with Jesus in communion with God in creation, I have suggested in the previous chapters that women must do three things. They need to accept themselves as women, as God's daughters and therefore sacred, thereby avoiding the temptation to believe that women are somehow immature, weak and incomplete by nature. They need to bond with other women and, in doing so, claim with pride the heritage that is ours which the world has typically denigrated: the values of care, empathy, cooperation, relationship, nurturing. And they need to develop spiritual practices that support the true self, not the self the world has carved out for us.

Speaking for the Self

For women, the pattern of alienation has been represented by silence. Far too often women's stories have been passed over in favor of other stories or have been told from the male perspective. Think of how relatively few women are represented in the Bible, in the pages of history books and chronicles of nations, in the leadership of the Church.

Only the powerful speak in the world. Several years ago a popular television commercial claimed that when a particular stockbroker talks, everyone listens. Money talks. Power talks. Fame and prestige talk. And while these voices clamor for attention, the poor, the weak, the unknown go unnoticed. So often silence is imposed on individuals or groups because they lack the power to make themselves heard.

Sometimes, however, the silence is self-imposed because of fear, shame or misplaced guilt. Maya Angelou stopped her voice while only a child because she blamed herself for the brutal death of the man who raped her. In her mind, she believed that if she had not told her family of the crime her mother's boyfriend had committed against her, someone would not have beaten him senseless. By naming the enemy, she had led to his destruction. She learned that words have power to create and to destroy. She stopped talking.

But swallowing one's words can also destroy; unuttered, they fester within until they infect and weaken the spirit. Angelou's autobiography, *I Know Why the Caged Bird Sings,* records how she once again found her voice—both literally and figuratively by writing the autobiography—and in doing so, found herself.

As a naïve young writing teacher many years ago, I let my students write about whatever topic they chose: joyous memories as well as deaths of loved ones, alcohol binges which resulted in terrible acts, parental rejection, rape, incest. I thank God that, despite my inexperience and youthful optimism, I instinctively knew not to try to offer counsel or pathetic words of consolation. I simply accompanied my students through the writing process—how to shape the narrative, how to use metaphor to reveal what was too horrible to them to state directly, how to develop a character. The weeks during this writing process were extremely difficult for the students, of course, who wrestled with the memories, and I always wondered why they chose such painful topics. But the weeks were also extremely difficult for me, who helplessly watched and felt almost cruel for remaining professionally detached. However, the resulting essays were remarkable. Yet what I found more remarkable was that these students thanked me for allowing them to explore such topics in a college class. Why the gratitude for pain? Yes, speaking one's pain can sometimes be cathartic. However, I don't think that was what was going on here. It was as if shaping that horrible experience into something which could be offered to strangers gave it meaning and order and purpose. The pain was no longer random and chaotic and valueless.

Perhaps that is why I have grown to love literature so deeply, and to love even more the process of creating. Words *are* powerful. "Let there be," God says in Genesis. At a word, creation exists. At a word, the bread and wine become Christ's body and blood. At a word, God becomes flesh (John 1:14). The Word is God.

Therefore, for me, to be in solidarity with God's creation means that I learn to listen to all the words of creation: the voice of the powerful who think that only by keeping up the din can they assure themselves of their value and worth, and the still small voice of the weak which can be heard in the silence. And I must learn to listen to my own voice because I am creation also.

The Widow Before the Judge

Finding the voice to speak of our pain, of our identity, and of that which prevents us from being what we are meant to be is often extremely difficult and frightening. It requires much courage, especially if we are not heard—if we are ignored or rebuked or criticized or punished. Such was the case in Jesus' parable of the widow before the corrupt judge. She lacks the influence to "play the game" the way it is played in this judge's court. She is too poor or unwilling to pay him the bribe that will prompt him to find in her favor. Yet she repeatedly appears before him, certain of the righteousness of her case, certain of her ability to make that righteousness apparent, certain of the judge's authority and power, certain that justice will prevail.

As the readers of the parable, we know justice will prevail. The narrative structure of the parable demands such a solution, and we also expect it because the judge's role is to protect those who need special protection like widows and orphans. Most likely, she is in a desperate financial situation because her opponent has taken advantage of her now that her husband is dead. Perhaps she has lost the inheritance that she needs to live. Therefore, we are not surprised when the judge finally grants the widow's petition. What does surprise us is why. The judge does not undergo a conversion whereby he realizes that he should fear God and respect humanity. In fact, he cares not for the rightness of the case, nor the plight of the widow, nor even that justice be done. So why does he change his mind? He is weary of her. He will grant what she asks simply to be rid of her. He also suspects that a person that dedicated to achieving a goal will not stop until the goal is achieved, perhaps causing him harm in the process. Perhaps the whole situation has become an embarrassment to him, setting him up as an object of ridicule or at least amusement before his peers. Perhaps he's afraid others will inquire into why she is dissatisfied and find out he is corrupt. Perhaps some will rally to her defense and threaten him physically.

Although the parable purports to be about God's justice, the focus of the parable is really the woman's persistent petitioning. She is shameless. Remember that women without men to protect and speak for them were without honor in this culture. Any respectable woman would not have continually exposed herself to public shame by going alone so often before the judge. Yet who else will do it for her? The judge is her only hope. On his decision rests her fate—not only whether she wins or loses her case, and thus lives in prosperity or destitute poverty, but also whether the judge will become her patron, remove her shame and restore her honor. Therefore, the parable is not really about justice but about something else. The widow's action becomes a metaphor for the coming of the kingdom. The kingdom keeps coming, wearing resistance down, regardless of honor or even justice. It may even come in the guise of shamelessness.

When I think back over the times I have felt compelled to speak out—in defense of a project in danger of being eliminated, or against some injustice done to me or another, or merely offering my experience as an example of some truth I am teaching—I am struck by the feeling of shamelessness that came over me. In each case where I have had to address my superiors, I felt at the time that I was being disrespectful and impertinent, if not impolite. They were, after all, in positions of authority for good reason. They had more power, knowledge of the situation, intelligence and experience, or so I thought. In those cases where I offered my personal experience to my students or readers, I afterwards felt embarrassed, as if I had committed some indecency or gaffe in propriety. In both situations, I didn't feel worthy or able enough to speak well. I hoped in vain for someone else to champion the cause and explicate the truth. I even suspected that I might be doing more harm than good. On those few occasions where I was ignored or rebuked for speaking out, I began to doubt myself: Perhaps I had been wrong, after all. Perhaps my motives were not as clear as I had thought. Perhaps I had misread or misconstrued the facts. Perhaps I had no business speaking out.

If the widow had remained silent, she would have remained respectable, but alienated. She would have been alienated from herself—her needs, desires, values, abilities. She would have been alienated from others—those who did not even see her in the community because they were involved with their own concerns, those who refused her as did the judge, those who even abused her such as her opponent. She would have been alienated from God—from righteousness and goodness and justice and mercy. By finding her voice and risking dishonor, she became the tool for God's inbreaking kingdom.

We cannot keep silent.

Yet we find it extremely difficult to speak. Let me offer some guidelines to help us find our true voices.

1. Sorting Truth From Falsehood

When I reflect about the stories that comprise my life, I am dismayed at how ready I am to cast myself in the role of righteous victor or innocent victim. Or, when that is impossible, how quickly I can rationalize my decisions. Unfortunately, I have not found my response unique, but have witnessed it repeatedly in the stories others tell me of their lives. One such storyteller is Daisy Goodwill Flett in Carol Shields' novel *Stone Diaries.* Daisy's narration of her life does not coincide with the facts Shields presents us, allowing Shields to explore the human inclination to mask our identity, recreate our identity, even construct the reality we experience. In order to hold on to our lives, Daisy claims, we feel we must rescue them by using our imagination to alter or add to our experiences, to see connections or reasons for events, even to invent or obviously lie about what happened, what was said, what was meant. Yet all the while we believe these deceptions are the truth because of the positive light they cast upon us.

Given this human condition, it is a wonder really that we can ever remove the curtain under which we shroud our true motivations and desires. We are all too willing to tolerate the darkness instead of welcoming the light, all too willing to abdicate responsibility instead of owning our choices and actions, all too willing to see ourselves as passive victims of circumstances instead of active participants in life. We become, as Daisy writes, someone "who's learned to dig a hole in her own life story."

Carroll Saussy, after conducting surveys and interviews of seminarians where she teaches, became suspicious that what some call faith in God is really an escape from faith in self. She writes in *God Images and Self-Esteem:*

> *What many women and men call faith in God is an escape from the need to establish a foundational belief in their own value and destiny and in their own innate capacity to respond to the challenges of life. Faith is too often used as*

> *a life preserver for people who are not sure they can really swim. Too many TV evangelists have connected religious faith with material success, health cures, and personal aggrandizement. Some students, too, talk about the connection between their religious faith and the experience of success or cures or special protection from illness or death. A rare few speak of discovering the incarnate Deity in themselves, of finding themselves empowered to respond to their own problems.*[1]

When we can accept that we have the power within us to control and shape our responses to "problems," then we will also have the power to resist, like Jesus, the temptation the devil offers to take over our lives for us. Worship me, the tempter says, and I will take care of the rest; I will assume all responsibility; I will make those difficult moral decisions for you. We are sorely tempted because we are so afraid that we might make the wrong decision, do the wrong thing, believe the wrong statement. We dare not trust ourselves. We dare not trust that God will forgive us for making a wrong decision. What Saussy discovered is true: We lack faith.

Therefore, the first step toward finding our voices is to sort through the rationalizations and lies we have layered around ourselves. We have to acknowledge our own responsibility for our lives.

Saussy says that the trap that ensnared the women on this journey toward responsibility in her study is "the assumption that if they could be good enough to win the unqualified approval of another, they would achieve their goal in life. Being good enough, however, came to mean achieving perfection" (p. 100). Perfection means different things for different women. For one it might mean acceptance by everyone she works with; for another, success in all she attempts; for another, a beautiful body, or saving her parents' troubled marriage, or having children who excel in school. "As long as one needs perfection in order to arrive at unqualified approval," Saussy argues, "one must live in anxiety that the imperfection one well knows to be part of her life might be discovered" (p. 100). Many have the misunderstanding that only by being good enough, by being perfect, can they win God's approval. Jesus reminds us that God does not demand this of us. When one of his interviewers called him good, Jesus replied, "Why do you call me good? No one is good but God alone" (18:19 *NRSV*).

Therefore, to be responsible for oneself means that the criterion for judgment must shift from goodness to truth. Earlier we mentioned Carol Gilligan's studies of women's moral development and how women base their decisions on the value of care. Moral dilemmas arise in situations of conflict where no matter what decision the woman makes someone will be hurt. Simple and clear solutions are impossible because, since humans are connected in an elaborate network of relationships, the fact that someone is hurt affects everyone who is involved. Moral dilemmas are dilemmas precisely because they involve conflicting responsibilities.

Gilligan asserts that moral growth occurs when a woman views the conflict not as a threat but as a normal outgrowth of living in relationship. She must overcome the notion that selfishness and responsibility are in opposition, and instead make a decision with care, on the basis of her knowledge, her ability to see other possible solutions and her willingness to own the choice she makes from those possible solutions. This is, of course, much easier to say than to do.

Women have a particular problem answering the question of responsibility. They are quick to blame others for failing to meet their needs: for failing to fill up their emptiness or to provide them with happiness and love. Yet, at the same time, they are all too quick to accept blame for everything that happens to those around them. We assume guilt for other people's problems and believe that if we just try hard enough, we can solve or at least avert their problems.

The question of responsibility becomes even more complicated—for both women and men—when no one can be held responsible. One of our most sacred and fundamental delusions is the belief that the world is just. When faced with obvious injustice, we have to find a reason, a cause, for the injustice, even when there is none. Research has shown that when no clear cause can be attributed for the injustice, people tend to denigrate the victim, deny the evidence or reinterpret the event. Some people will even blame themselves for the injustice rather than accept the unsettling conclusion that no one is responsible. By blaming themselves, they feel that they can regain control of the situation. "If I caused this," they say to themselves, "then I can take steps in the future to avoid it." If no one is to blame, then there is no order, logic, justice. That, for most of us, is intolerable.

Interestingly enough, our response to personal injustice follows fairly identifiable stages. The first, of course, is the personal experience itself—let's say a woman's discovery that she was hired at a lesser salary than a male colleague to do a similar job. The individual's reaction to the experience is often confused, contradictory or unarticulated. She may rationalize the situation by deciding that their jobs really are not the same, or that skills and experience are different enough to warrant his greater pay. But then she feels she works harder than he does. She may remind herself that she shouldn't be so concerned about money, that her own sense of worth or her employer's and coworkers' respect for her abilities are far more important. Yet salary is a validation of performance. She may experience anger and frustration with her employers—at the same time that she desires to please them. She may be depressed and wonder why. And, of course, there's the male colleague: How does she feel toward him?

The second stage is the realization that injustice has occurred and that there are alternatives to the present course of action. What follows, surprisingly, is not anger, but embarrassment and humiliation. The woman berates herself for being so stupid and for letting "them" do this to her. If only she had been more aggressive during the negotiation stage when she was hired. If only she had the courage to confront her employers now. If only she was strong enough to look for another job.

The third stage is when the individual shifts the blame from self to another. This often results in anger, which makes this stage a very difficult period to live through. We only feel anger when we see the hope for change. Anger gives us a feeling of power (and group support often generates anger because of the power one feels when supported by others). If the individual is able to successfully negotiate this stage without becoming bogged down in anger—or the indirect expressions of anger such as depression, emotional distancing, self-destruction, boredom—then she will begin to realize that her "opponent" was not malicious or misguided, but was in fact trying to live out the expectations of his or her role.

Therefore, the last stage is the effort to discriminate between what can and cannot be done in the particular situation. Keep in mind that, because we're in relationship, our behavior supports the behavior of others. We can't change others, but we can change ourselves. Perhaps we could set limits to what we will allow others to ask of us. We could stop rescuing our bosses, coworkers or spouses so that they do not have to face the consequences of their own behavior. We could refuse to allow the Church to trivialize women's experiences. We could make sure that our donations go to women's projects. We could ourselves offer time, energy and talents to programs which reclaim women's ability to contribute to society—by working in a woman's shelter, or tutoring women students, or conducting biblical research to reclaim women's spiritual practices. Keep in mind, too, that others may resist this new behavior of ours. If we are not prepared, their resistance can surprise or even defeat us.

In order to gain greater personal responsibility through these stages, Harriet Lerner in *The Dance of Anger* suggests three steps. First, she recommends that we practice careful observation. What were the sequences of events and interactions that led up to the event? How did we manage our response? How did others respond to us? Second, she tells us to clarify the pattern of behavior. Who was all too willing to underfunction and play the passive role? Who was all too willing to overfunction? To be able to discern these patterns, we must make a conscious effort to be less reactive to the situation and more able to focus our attention on what is happening. Finally, she encourages us to gather data. How does the pattern we discerned relate to our own family or community traditions over the generations? How have others responded to similar circumstances and with what results? What other options are available for dealing with the situation or for dealing with the emotions the situation arouses?

2. Dealing With Anger

Because anger is one of the dominant emotions aroused during this process of finding our voices, we would do well to understand this often misunderstood emotion. Although most of us have been taught that anger should be avoided at all costs, it is not in itself a bad thing. All emotions are neither good nor evil, but are our natural, God-given responses to stimuli. It's how we choose to act from the emotion that can be judged as good or evil. Anger is actually a very healthy state that lets us know when our sense of justice or fairness or our well-being has been violated. If, for instance, we feel chronically angry about a significant relationship to us, what that signals is that we have compromised too much of the self and are uncertain about what the next step should be. To feel angry is not a weakness but a call to acknowledge our own lack of clarity in the relationship. Anger, therefore, signals the need for a change, and if we can channel it so that we do right the injustice or restore the balance of fairness or grow into more responsible individuals, we find the anger not only healthy but useful.

Although feeling anger may signal a problem, venting anger never solves it. Despite what many pop psychology gurus may say, venting anger only serves to maintain the problem situation. Virginia Woolf, for instance, complained in *A Room of One's Own* that women writers who gave way to anger produced only weak writing, not the changes they wanted. High emotional intensity often leads to nonproductive efforts to change another person rather than using our power to change ourselves. An angry outburst may draw attention to an abuse, but that is about all it accomplishes. Real change requires discernment, organization, patience, good humor and the ability to negotiate and compromise. Woolf herself writes splendidly out of anger because she transcends it. Anger becomes for her a source of creative energy. As Harriet Lerner writes, "Anger is a tool for change when it challenges us to become more of an expert on the self and less of an expert on others."[2]

We are not expected to make this change by ourselves. God will help us—if we turn over our anger to God. This was a lesson I learned after unsuccessfully wrestling with my feelings after an injustice had been committed against me by someone in the Church. For months I suffered alone, berating myself for not being able to forgive, frightening myself with unexpected surges of hatred and terrible dreams where I acted out my aggression while asleep. Finally I remembered those psalms that always made me uncomfortable, the ones where the psalmist prays that God will wreak unimaginable evils upon evildoers ("O God, break the teeth in their mouths.... Let them vanish like water that runs away" [Psalm 58:6, 7]). And how does the psalmist identify the evildoers? They are those who are against him, who thwart his plans and cause him harm, whether intentionally or not. One that particularly upset me has the psalmist asking God to destroy his enemy's children, just as the enemy had killed the children of his people ("Happy shall they be who pay you back what you have done to us! ...who take your little ones and dash them against the rock!" [Psalm 137:8-9 *NRSV]*). Only after I had experienced my own unresolved aggression did I understand the psalmist. No, I did not want to act out my revenge because I did not want to become the kind of person who would do so. But I wanted God to do it for me, to right the wrong, to make the other person suffer as I had suffered, to restore the balance of justice in my world. To hide my feelings was impossible. God knows them even before I am fully aware of them. To pray my feelings seemed unchristian but was not really so. I was, finally, acknowledging them, owning them and I was giving them to God. Only then was I ready for change. God transformed my feelings of anger and hatred ever so slowly until after months I realized I no longer hated, that I could in fact pray for the person who had harmed me. To have remained silent, to have bottled my emotions and desires inside, would have further alienated me from this person—as well as further alienating me from my own feelings and from God who seemed impassive and insensitive to my plight.

Popular wisdom has told us that women have a greater problem with anger than men. Just think of the adjectives used to describe an angry man compared to those for a woman. In fact, an angry man is often considered to be assertive and strong, while an angry woman is "bitchy" or overbearing. However, research into anger reveals that men and women do not differ in their readiness to be angry, but in their willingness to express anger. And when researchers examine the social environment, what they discover is that sex is *not* a factor in anger expression, but the position of power is. Women are just as willing to express anger at home as men—at their children, their aging parents, their spouses. (Wife abuse may command more attention than husband abuse, but it's because men tend to resort to closed fists, knives or guns while women slap, kick or punch. Therefore, men inflict greater damage.) Men are just as reluctant to express anger in public situations—especially at work with superiors—as women. Sex is not a factor in anger, therefore, but status is. Because women occupy, on average, lower positions in the social and economic structure, their expression of anger is more problematic. As a result, they turn the anger inward, into depression, apathy or cynicism; or they deny the anger, becoming "hurt" instead; or they displace the anger onto a third party or themselves.

3. Speaking in Ways That Will Be Heard

Because women fear anger so much, when they do speak out, their speech becomes very tentative, suggesting to their listeners that they do not take responsibility for their statements. Women frequently use qualifiers in their sentences, thereby lessening the impact of their conclusions. They often introduce statements of conviction with "I believe" or "I think," instead of "I know." They tend to use many questions, or end sentences with a rising inflection, as if unsure of the validity of what they are saying. They are concerned about how their hearer responds, frequently seeking approval either in gesture or word, changing their style depending on whether they get that approval. Their speech is often self-effacing if not self-deprecating.

These are, actually, characteristics of immature writers and thinkers. My freshman composition students exhibit the same traits. Because they are not yet assured of their convictions and their power to express those convictions, they write as if they automatically assume that I will correct, criticize or reject what they are saying. "This is just my opinion," a student will write, as if that exonerates her from being accountable for her statements. "This is how I saw it," another will write, as if that somehow releases him from trying to get at the truth of the situation. I am not to be taken seriously, such essays seem to say; I am merely a student who doesn't know much about the world of knowledge and thought yet. I am not to be taken seriously, much of women's speech seems to say; I am merely a woman who lacks power and prestige.

In order to help my students learn to write more effectively, we practice the steps given earlier for discerning the truth of a situation. We study carefully the factors involved in a particular act of communication: Who is the audience? What are the peculiar facts of the subject? What is the writer's purpose? What is the most effective medium for this subject with this audience? Then we clarify the pattern of the student's past errors and successes. What has worked before and why? What failed and why? And we gather as much information as we can about the writing process and about how other authors have approached similar problems. The same steps could be used for any situation, whether one is trying to write an essay for a college course, argue a case before one's superiors, arrive at a decision with one's spouse or understand how one thinks about an experience.

Some have argued that women and men find it difficult to communicate with one another because they are socialized into different patterns of reacting to the world. Women tend to listen more and share feelings, primarily because they want to use conversation to maintain relationships and avoid conflict. Men tend to use conversation competitively to find out who has the power and who does not. Men tend to lecture, and talk of facts and opinions instead of feelings. One popular author has even suggested that men and women are so different that it seems they came from different planets! However, as we saw with anger, these communication differences are not so much a result of sex but of social status. Men who are in low-status and powerless positions also use conversation to reduce conflict and remain connected, and tend to communicate indirectly. Women in high-status, powerful positions use conversation to maintain their position and engage in conflict, and tend to communicate directly.

My point is not that women should become more like men in order to command the respect higher-status positions afford. In fact, women's style of communication often makes them more effective spiritual directors and mentors. They have the ability to listen and offer help on the other's terms, encouraging growth and independence. A male spiritual director often offers help on *his* terms, fostering dependence. My point is that we have allowed our status position to control not only how we express ourselves but also what we express. If a woman is to understand who she is, she must find and speak with her own voice. She may not have the power to control what happens to her, but she does have the power to control how she will interpret an event, how she understands her feelings, how she thinks, how she responds. Ultimately that is true for all humans, regardless of gender. High status positions give merely the illusion of power. True power comes from within, from touching the divine spark that resides in each of us. When a woman finds her voice, she, like the widow in Jesus' parable, is able to speak words of divine power to worldly power, words of justice to corruption, of truth to illusion.

Barbara Kerr, in *Smart Girls (Revised Edition),* offers a list of ten communication skills developed by Linda Lee-Boesl, a teacher in a girls' school. Called "Rules for Real Women," they are worth reading carefully and practicing faithfully. When real women communicate:

1. They do not preface their opinions with self-effacing comments that dismiss the seriousness of their ideas.
2. They do not over-qualify their ideas in order to avoid taking responsibility for them.
3. They do not distract others with nervous mannerisms or irrelevant "chatter," and they make a point of looking the person in the eye, even, occasionally, calling him or her by name.
4. They do not speak too quickly or drop their voices at the end of a sentence in order to obscure their meaning; they avoid murmuring and whispering.

5. They do not apologize for holding an opinion that does not agree with others, and they do not expect others to convert to theirs. Their "goal" remains understanding, not "consensus."

6. They do not take responsibility for another's silence, for they realize that silence is often a respectful and creative response to understanding.

7. They do not interrupt the other person, and they avoid monopolizing the conversation.

8. They do not avoid asking questions about that which they have genuine doubt; neither do they ask superfluous ones about which they have *no* doubt.

9. They learn to listen "actively" by occasionally reflecting on the other's meanings; they make a sincere effort to truly hear.

10. They do not pretend to know something when, in fact, they do not. It is acceptable not to know; it is misleading to pretend otherwise. Neither do they feign ignorance.[3]

Notice how all of these rules invite both the speaker and the listener to unite in the search for common understanding. These rules respect the uniqueness of each individual's style and abilities, yet affirm that communion is possible.

Yes, words are powerful. They can alienate or bring together, spin lies or unveil the truth. They can destroy or create. Therefore, finding our voices is a blessed undertaking—and an awesome responsibility.

Questions for Reflection and Discussion

- *Consider a specific moral dilemma you personally faced. What were the factors that made it a dilemma for you? How did you resolve it, or did you? Try to list the steps you used in working through the problem. Describe the process you went through.*

- *Have you ever felt compelled to speak out—either to defend someone, point out an injustice or explain yourself? What compelled you? What was the experience like? How did you feel about yourself, the situation, your audience?*

- *Think of a particular incident when you felt that you suffered some injustice. Explain how your response did or did not follow the four stages listed on pages 97-98.*

- *Read Luke's account of Jesus cleansing the temple (19:45-46). Describe Jesus' attitude and actions. What is your reaction to this story?*

- *Read Psalms 58 and 109. What is your reaction to these cries for vengeance? Would you call these prayers? Why or why not? Should we pray our "negative" as well as our "positive" desires?*

- *What makes you angry? Don't simply focus on particular circumstances that have happened to you, but attempt to draw some conclusion about the kinds of things that arouse anger in you. For instance, I often become angry when I discover I've been discriminated against, or when others presume to speak for me (such as when my husband volunteers me for a project without first asking me).*

- *How do you deal with anger? How do others respond to you when you are angry? How do you feel about yourself afterward?*

Notes

[1] Carroll Saussy. *God Images and Self-Esteem: Empowering Women in a Patriarchal Society* (Louisville, Ky.: Westminster John Knox Press, 1991), pp. 13-14.

[2] Harriet Goldhor Lerner, Ph.D. *The Dance of Anger: A Woman's Guide to Changing the Patterns of Intimate Relationships* (New York: Harper & Row, 1985), p. 102.

[3] Barbara Kerr, Ph.D. *Smart Girls (Revised Edition)*: A *New Psychology of Girls, Women, and Giftedness* (Scottsdale, Ariz.: Gifted Psychology Press, 1997), pp. 222-223.

CHAPTER EIGHT

A Woman's Place Is in the Home

Activity: *Using magazine clippings, snapshots or mementos, construct a collage illustrating your family's structure. (You may consider your family at present, or in the past when your children were younger, or your own childhood family.) Some questions to consider: How does your family make decisions, assign chores, mediate conflict, allocate resources such as money, food, time and clothing? Is the power in your family centralized or shared by several individuals? What means does your family employ to assure the cooperation of its members? How is punishment decided and carried out?*

As you have probably guessed by now, I love metaphor and symbol. Language theorists claim our first thoughts as infants were images. For many adults, thoughts are still primarily visual. Therefore, for much that we know and experience we have no words. How does one talk about love, freedom, God? Words seem inadequate. So we devise metaphors: God as father, mother, fire, wind, light, bridegroom, the Word made flesh. Metaphor and symbol come as close to expressing these truths as anything we have.

Luke loved metaphor and symbol, too. Recall his symbolic use of healing and eating, among many others. Part of Luke's great genius is his ability to use our basic experiences to express God's salvation. Another set of symbols Luke uses is just as basic, and therefore rich in meaning and experience for his audience: the temple and the household.

In chapter after chapter, Jesus moves from village to village, speaking in local synagogues, visiting homes, encountering people where they live and work and die. As the tension builds between the Jewish authorities and Jesus, Luke has Jesus approach Jerusalem, until in the climactic chapters Jesus denounces the temple as a den of thieves, and the authorities plot and execute his death. At Jesus' death, the temple veil is torn asunder. Luke's Acts also establishes the Christian ministry in tension with the temple authorities. The early disciples teach in local homes and synagogues and establish house churches. The Jewish authorities accuse Jesus' followers of abandoning the customs of their ancestors. When Stephen is seized and brought before the council, the Jews complain, "This man never stops saying things against [this] holy place and the law. For we have heard him claim that this Jesus the Nazorean will destroy this place and change the customs that Moses handed down to us" (Acts 6:13-14). When Paul visits James in Jerusalem, the Jerusalem Christians worry about the Jewish reaction to Paul's ministry: "Brother, you see how many thousands of believers there are from among the Jews, and they are all zealous observers of the law. They have been informed that you are teaching all the Jews who live among the Gentiles to abandon Moses and that you are telling them not to circumcise their children or observe their customary practices. What is to be done?" (Acts 21:20-22).

What is to be done? Luke presents Jesus and his disciples as not walking in the way of God. It seems as if Jesus has abandoned the customs of their ancestors. Luke sets up this conflict by placing in opposition two settings: the household and village, where Jesus is found most often, and the temple, where Jesus is rejected. What is to be done with all these contrasting references to the locale of God's saving work?

Home and Temple

By the time Luke is writing, the Romans have already destroyed Jerusalem and its glorious temple. We find it difficult to understand how devastating this conquest was for the Jews and for the Jewish Christians, as well as for the gentiles in Luke's audience who had earlier converted to Judaism before Christianity. The temple was the center of all Jewish life—not just its religious center, but its political and economic center as well. Here was the central control for the storage and redistribution of surplus agricultural goods. Here was the nation's treasury, inflated with sacrifice offerings, temple taxes and tithes, used for the upkeep of not only the temple but also the production and distribution of resources and services. Here was where debts were recorded. Here was where the Sanhedrin met, the court that codified rabbinic law, as well as handled census, taxation and other administrative responsibilities, and maintained the Jewish military. Here also rested the Jewish trust and hope in God's promises. Had not God promised to dwell in this holy city? Had not God assured them that Jerusalem would be the light for the entire world, where Jew and gentile alike would come to do homage? Therefore, when the walls fell, they sent shock waves through the entire Jewish nation.

Those who survived fled to Jewish communities spread throughout the Roman Empire, and the Jews began the painful process of reevaluating their religious, social and political culture now that the center of that culture was gone.

Luke's message is that the center was already lost to many before Rome besieged it. The temple had fallen under the control of powerful, wealthy families—of the chief priests, the elders and Herod's bureaucrats—who increased their land holdings and power under Roman occupation by burdening the people with tremendous taxes and debts. More and more peasants found themselves unable to pay and sold their family lands or even sold their family members into slavery. The entire social structure of the villages, based on cooperative labor and social reciprocity, was being undermined, and the poor and powerless—once protected by the Law—were now being exploited by the keepers of the Law. Many a household that once had the resources to care for its own was broken apart with its members becoming dependent on handouts and alms from the rich attending at temple.

Not only did the powerful exclude many from the political and economic life, but also from the religious life of the temple. Temple worship was based on a system of purity that ultimately excluded many. As we have seen, race, sex, occupation, disease, accident, natural bodily functions and social status could all label a person as unclean, and therefore possibly unworthy of offering sacrifice or even participating in the religious life at all.

Luke establishes the temple as a metaphor for the opposite of kingdom values. The temple was an institution of primarily political significance, where power was centralized, wealth and resources redistributed from local sources to Jerusalem, and projects accomplished by coercion and economic exploitation. Rather than welcoming all, it excluded and alienated many deemed "impure," and organized itself around a strict hierarchy. It was, as Jesus points out, a spiritually bankrupt system enamored with wealth and power, a veritable den of thieves.

Home and Kingdom

Luke's Jesus envisioned a more domestic community as his model for the kingdom. The domestic household is an institution based on kinship, in which all are welcomed and accepted simply because they are family or guests. A nation comprised of households would have less centralized power, and projects would thus more likely be accomplished by members' commitment to one another and by cooperative sharing. Goods and services would be exchanged based on their availability and members' needs. Members are included based on relationship, and conflicts resolved through repentance, justice and mercy. Ranking of members is based on their roles within the family, and authority is traditional, not bureaucratic. For Jesus, the household was an apt symbol for the dwelling place of the Spirit, a place where all are brothers and sisters because they are children of God. The household is a world of table fellowship and service, of generosity, familial faith and loyalty, repentance and forgiveness, justice and mercy, friendship, intimacy and solidarity.

In short, it is a world of love and compassion.

As women discover their political voice, they need to remember the danger of restoring the temple as the means of salvation, of looking toward an institution to support the human qualities Jesus advocates. We must keep these two sets of sometimes opposing values clearly before us, so that we can, like the disciples, be careful of the old way that may sometimes lead to corruption and death, and follow the new way. A woman's place *is* in the "home," as is everyone's place. Women and children have traditionally had more autonomy, respect and authority within the home setting than in the public setting, so we are apt champions for the values associated with the household. In Jesus' day, women would have been responsible for household management. Their male relatives may have held the power of decision, but women had the administrative power. Women regulated the studies, the occupation and the recreation of children, even of the male children until they came of age. Women were responsible for food and clothing production, storage and distribution of goods within the family, the supervision and training of servants, perhaps even the field servants. Some maintained cottage industries, and as businesswomen (like Lydia in Acts 16) would have traveled, traded and negotiated contracts. There is some evidence that they even read and studied the Torah—

but only in the privacy of the household.

Keep in mind, however, that this "home" we are discussing is not necessarily a specific locale but is the symbolic representation of the kingdom Jesus inaugurated. Home is our spiritual center and source, where we find nourishment, rest and meaningful work. Home is also the space we share with others in solidarity and compassion. Home is the kingdom.

If we are to be effective champions of the "home team," we need to channel our efforts in two areas. We need, first of all, to confront the current power structures of our patriarchal culture, the bankrupt "temple culture" which no longer serves. Then we need to examine and change our patterns of relating to power—both individually and collectively as a society.

Confront Current Power Structures

Conflict is a dirty word for many women. Conflict means tension, disharmony, perhaps anger, danger, even violence—all difficult for women who feel they are supposed to be mediators and soothers. Such women are made to feel that something is wrong with them if they feel conflict. Let's don't talk about actually engaging in it.

However, conflict is an inevitable part of living in relationships and is actually necessary for growth. Disagreements often force us to clarify our beliefs and values, reassess our actions, uncover our motives. Most of us rarely examine our lives, and merely respond to the daily cycle of events to which we have grown accustomed—until a crisis occurs. As a result of the crisis, we may break a cycle of passivity or dysfunctional responses that impede the way of further development. Although conflict is seen as dangerous, failing to see the need for conflict and failing to provide appropriate forms for it actually lead to danger. We may, however, experience a period of depression and disorganization while we work through the conflict. It is as if we are mourning the person we once were—

no matter how immature, unthinking or careless that person was. However, real self-destruction can result from trying to avoid or suppress conflict, as we saw earlier in our discussion of the development of adolescent girls in our male-oriented society.

Yet this society is not serving men well either. Power-hungry, materialistic, consumeristic, individualistic, our culture is, as Pope John Paul II declares, a culture of death. In his *Evangelium Vitae (The Gospel of Life),* he argues that we are living in a climate of widespread moral uncertainty, in which we confuse good and evil, which has led to the breakdown of the social and family structure. Several roots have nourished this problem. One is that our modern culture has exalted humans as autonomous beings with no dependence on others. Another is that we have equated personal dignity with the capacity for success, denying the value of handicapped or otherwise marginalized individuals. We have separated truth from freedom, making our point of reference the subjective person, rather than universal and objective truth. We have, in great numbers, embraced relativism. We have adopted materialism, which leads to individualism, utilitarianism and hedonism. In such a world, suffering has no meaning and should be avoided at all cost. Our culture has eclipsed the sense of God and of the human, especially of humanity's dignity and need for conversion. Humans are not seen as any different from other creatures, although more highly developed. Humans are perceived as things rather than gifts. And the whole notion of a transcendent character, of a soul and spirituality, is discounted.

When Jesus approached Jerusalem, he wept. "If you, even you, had only recognized on this day the things that make for peace!" he cried, and his words are meant for the worldly cultures of today.

> *But now they are hidden from your eyes. Indeed, the days will come upon you, when your enemies will set up ram-*

> *parts around you and surround you, and hem you in on every side. They will crush you to the ground, you and your children within you, and they will not leave within you one stone upon another; because you did not recognize the time of your visitation from God.* (Luke 19:42-44, NRSV)

Immediately after these words, Jesus cleanses the temple area. To be a Christian means that we will inevitably and necessarily come in conflict with the "temple culture."

We can develop strategies to deal effectively with the conflict. In a culture of power, the weak still have power they can claim. They can refuse to believe what the culture tells them. A woman can refuse to accept the culture's definition of who she is as a person, of what her role is to be. This is the first step toward imagining alternatives and liberty. The weak, who are often separate and alone, also have the power to come together for confirmation and support. The Spirit will be in their midst. A community can help a woman understand herself and her position, and it can help her deal with the distress and conflicts resulting from her new perspectives. Finally the weak, in community, can act in common pursuit of shared goals.

Change Patterns of Relating to Power

Unfortunately, women often shun the direct action needed to accomplish goals, because they believe both politics and power are evil. They would do well to remember the story of the shameless widow and the corrupt judge. The story reminds us that we can redefine power. Instead of viewing it as a quality possessed only by a single individual, we can view power as a process of interaction between several individuals. The traditional definition of power as unilateral considers it a sign of weakness to be influenced by another. Individuals are judged by whether or not they can resist or overthrow others' competing power. No wonder women find power so distasteful; we are usually the losers in such a competition. We either are unsuccessful in claiming power from another or, if successful, feel that we have gained at the expense of another. Either way, we feel we have lost. But if we define power as mutual influence, then any increase of power by one person does not mean that the other loses power. We should not talk about "dividing" power and giving some to women in certain spheres where they didn't have it before. Rather we should talk about entering into a partnership that affirms the dignity and worth of all partners. Power may lead to collaboration, and produce rather than competition real change in both parties.

Think for a minute of how power is lived out in the home. Children, although weaker and more vulnerable members of the family, are anything but powerless. Even an infant can communicate its needs and have them met. Family life often revolves around the schedules of all the members: the children's school activities, father's and mother's work schedules. In relationships, power is ideally used to foster growth that ultimately removes the initial disparity or inequality. A parent nurtures a child, in turn being nurtured by caring for that child, until he is ready to become an adult and make his own decisions. A teacher educates the student, learning as much or more from the student in the process, until they are colleagues. In relationships, power is ideally not a matter of dominance and submission, but a true marriage of individuals.

In any social unit there are leaders and there are those who are led. Viewing power as mutual influence does not and should not change that fact. What it does change is our understanding of what it means to be a leader. It does not mean dominance or superiority. And being the one who is led does not mean being submissive and inferior. Because any group diminishes to some extent the personal identity of its members, the problem is how to maintain the group identity without destroying the personal identity of each member. Both the leaders and the led play an important role in that dynamic.

Luke especially calls leaders to account since they face

the particularly strong temptation to dominate and deprive the led of their identities. When threatened, leaders may defend the traditions of the group and label others as the enemy. In Acts, Luke criticizes Herod, Pilate and the Jewish leaders for just this response (4:24-28). Or leaders may find ways to assimilate the threat into their own views. Luke warns the disciples against those who will distort truth in order to keep or entice followers (20:30).

Jesus represents the true leader. At the Last Supper, he reminds the twelve that those who possess power do not lord it over others but use it to serve others (22:24-27). As Jesus served them, becoming their very food in the bread and wine, so they are to serve the world, liberating captives from economic and social prisons not of their own making, calling for repentance from those who have chained themselves in sin.

The led, on the other hand, must not succumb to the temptation of servility. They must not slavishly adhere to tradition that prevents them from new perspectives and growth. They must not remain satisfied with things that give momentary pleasure or reprieve but forge chains for those who come after. And they must not give in to the fear that prevents them from speaking words of power to power.

Yes, Luke's ethic seems impractical. It has been over nineteen hundred years since he wrote his Gospel, and still the world is not one of kinship, integration, sharing and love. But to think that we alone can bring about these kingdom values is foolish, Luke says. We have once again slipped into the role of Martha and been led astray by worldly concepts of power, even if for a divine cause. Jesus is the source of our power. Jesus is the Liberator. Jesus is the Servant of all. Jesus is Salvation.

We are not.

Questions for Reflection and Discussion

- *If Jesus were to select your household as a model of kingdom values, what examples from your family life would he use to illustrate his points to the crowd?*
- *Do you separate the public and private spheres of your life? Explain. Has this ever limited your perspective?*
- *Describe a relationship you were a part of that exhibited power as mutual influence.*
- *How do you perceive the Church's use of power today, especially when compared to the early Christian community?*
- *How would you rate the Church's mission in confronting the dominant values of our culture? Would you agree that this is the Church's role? Why or why not?*
- *Does our economic system contribute to poverty, homelessness and hunger? How?*
- *Have you ever confronted a cultural institution as an advocate for change? What was the experience like?*
- *How do you hang onto your own ideas of what needs to be done when others want to keep the old system?*
- *Pick one of the values of the "culture of death": materialism, say, or relativism. How could you personally confront this value in order to effect change?*

Conclusion

In *Facing the Abusing God,* David Blumenthal writes:

> *To be a theologian is...to speak for God. It is to have a personal rapport with God, to have a sense of responsibility for God and for how God is understood and related to by our fellow human beings. It is to mediate between God, as one understands God, and those who listen. It is to create an echo of God in the other.*[1]

I read Blumenthal's words in Carroll Saussy's *The Gift of Anger: A Call to Faithful Action* after I had written the first draft of this book. They spoke powerfully to me for they captured what I had been feeling yet had not been able to express. I had never thought of myself as a theologian. In fact, I have felt rather incompetent, ill-equipped and ill-prepared to be a theologian. The task is awe-full, almost arrogant, it seems to me. How can one presume to speak for God?

Yet that is what a theologian does. To be a theologian is to speak for God, not of God. To be a theologian is to take responsibility for how God is understood. To be a theologian is to play the role of mediator between God and others.

Every time I have taught a Bible study session or led a Confirmation class or worked with catechumens or written another chapter for this book, I have felt an awesome responsibility to be accurate, open, honest—with the material, with my audience, with myself, with God. I have often come home after one of those programs or stood up from the computer wondering if I spoke for God or for me. Did I say what needed to be said, or did I say what *I* wanted to say? Did I use words that revealed God's glory, God's mercy, God's saving power, God's love? Or did I use words that revealed merely my skill or, worse yet, rationalized or explained away God's actions? Did my language acknowledge my own responsibility and freedom as God's creation, or did I make excuses for myself? How can I be sure that my audience understands me, let alone that I understand God? Theology can be a very dangerous business.

However, Saussy, who also believes theologies are dangerous, writes that "They can also offer grace-filled, life-giving, albeit limited perspectives, and they must be put forth tentatively and with modesty."[2] I cannot speak for my audience, but I can truly say that working on this book for these last many months has been a grace-filled, life-giving and humbling experience for me.

First, I have grown in my respect and love for Luke's writings, because one can truly encounter God in them. My journey led me to scholars who find in Luke a voice that seems sympathetic to women. Luke includes more women as characters in his stories than any of the other New Testament writers, and the frequency of Jesus' interaction with women has prompted many women readers to see in Luke an ally. Some scholars suspect that these additional stories came from a woman's source—a collection preserved or perhaps written by women about women's experiences of the Jesus movement. Some even wonder if the author was a woman who assumed a male persona in the work.

Then I discovered those scholars who have become highly critical of Luke's treatment of women once they analyzed what Luke did and did not say about women in comparison to what he said about men. Rather than seeing him as an ally, they see Luke as trying to educate and control women, limiting them to ministries of hospitality and almsgiving, silencing them from preaching the good news, and prohibiting them from missionary work. It is not that the Christian message is antithetical to women, these scholars say, but that women must read "against the grain" of the evangelist's androcentric message in order to recover the liberating message of the Good News for all people—whether gentile or Jew, free or slave, male or female.

The more I have studied Luke's stories about women in the context of the entire Gospel and the Gospel in the context of Luke's era, the more I realize that I can agree with neither side's assessment of Luke. To claim that we must somehow salvage Jesus' liberating message for women from beneath the tarnish of Luke's misogyny is certainly unfair and destructive to Luke's concerns and message. Yet to uncritically read him as a friend of women can also be unfair and destructive to women's spirituality and ministerial identity. Luke's major concern was not to address his Gospel to women, but to proclaim the Good News to all—men *and* women. He struggled between trying to meet the needs of women gentile converts and presenting an apology of the Christian movement that would be understood and accepted by his Roman-educated audience—an audience who had very definite ideas about the role of women in the family and in society at large.

When we turn our attention to Luke's proclamation of the Good News, we find that the "good news" is that God is a merciful benefactor who heaps benefits without regard to moral performance. Jesus showers those he meets with healing gifts, regardless of whether they are sinful or taboo or deserving of a good man's attentions. With story after story, Luke poses the question: How can we respond to this God? This is a God who gives grace regardless of what we do. This kind of God is truly great, truly awesome. This kind of God is thoroughly and completely liberating.

For Luke, the only acceptable response to God's liberating action in our lives is a revolution of our minds. To accept Jesus requires that we deeply probe ourselves to recognize what has limited and enslaved us, what has divided our loyalties, what has robbed us of our true identity as God's daughters and sons. Then we must revolt: We must put off that which enslaves us and accept God's freedom.

Luke shows us that we cannot evaluate women and men merely by external traits or events. We cannot even use their actions to evaluate their relationship with God. (Recall the parable of the Pharisee and the tax collector.) It is not the code of behavior that we have accepted that determines our salvation, but what is at the core of our being. Therefore, we must not give in to the temptation of turning Luke's writings into another code of behavior—what is and is not acceptable for Christian women (passivity and silence or prophecy and challenge?), what ministries are appropriate for women (hospitality or preaching?) and so on.

In the words of one of his critics, Luke's Gospel is "an extremely dangerous text," but not for the reasons she cites—which have to do with what she sees as his somewhat negative treatment of women. Rather his text is dangerous because revolutions are dangerous—and painful and shocking. Women can expect to be challenged by Luke. His stories should disturb and dissatisfy. They just may be about us personally.

And this leads me to the second grace-filled, life-giving and extremely humbling experience for me, although at the time, I thought it was anything but grace-filled! I began to feel that this entire project was about me personally, that I was being challenged. And I became disturbed and dissatisfied. The feeling began to surface as I was working with the cultural material for Part Two, "And the Angel Came to Her." I grew increasingly frustrated and angry—but at what I was not sure. Unfortunately, I blamed many other sources before I was able to pinpoint the cause many weeks after I finished that section, and it had to do with my own personal history as I reexamined it in light of what I was studying and writing about Luke.

I was not prepared for such an emotional response in

myself. Nothing I had written before had affected me so. Nor was I prepared for the emotional response within the group of women who reviewed these chapters for me. One woman told me that these chapters made her depressed. Depression can be an indirect expression of anger, and she mentioned that she was doing what I was doing—reexamining her past. Another woman tearfully remarked that she had never imagined that Christ could and would serve her. I felt powerless in the face of all these emotions, especially those within myself. I felt embarrassed and apologetic that something I had written had triggered such commotion within people, excited but fearful that my words were being taken seriously (for did I really know what I was doing?) and humbled by what I was witnessing. I was beginning to wonder about my own rapport with God—and with myself, for that matter. Is this what Blumenthal meant when he said theologians create an echo of God in the other?

Yes, I think so. Our experiences are a powerful witness to what Luke means by conversion and counting the cost of discipleship.

The third grace-filled, life-giving experience came through the people I worked with during these months, especially the women who "tried out" my ideas. They encouraged and nurtured me. They asked me to speak at other gatherings. Their questions and comments challenged me and offered new perspectives. In fact, this book grew from a woman's request that I talk about Luke's views on women. Luke, the evangelist with whom I have always struggled!

I have tried to accomplish what Blumenthal asks of a theologian. I prayerfully hope that your study of Luke will develop in you, as it did in me, a deeper, fuller relationship with God. I hope that I have made Luke not only accessible to women, but a clear and pressing call demanding your response. I hope that I have served as a mediator, opening my resources, my skills, my experiences to you in order to make God's action in our lives apparent if not understandable. And

I pray that God uses my voice—the voice I found as I worked through this process—to reverberate as an echo of God in you.

Notes

[1] Blumenthal, David. *Facing the Abusing God.* (Louisville, Ky.: Westminster John Knox Press, 1993).

[2] Saussy, Carroll. *The Gift of Anger: A Call to Faithful Action*, p. 66.

Suggestions for Further Reading

An asterisk (*) by an entry signals that this work will have particular appeal for the general reader.

Luke's Gospel and Acts: General Studies

*Apicella, Raymond. *Journeys Into Luke.* Cincinnati: St. Anthony Messenger Press, 1992.

Brown, Raymond E. *New Testament Essays.* Milwaukee, Wisc.: Bruce Publishing, 1965. See particularly, "The Beatitudes According to Luke," pp. 265-271.

*Danker, Frederick. *Luke.* Philadelphia: Augsburg Fortress Press, 1976.

Gillman, John. *Possessions and the Life of Faith.* Collegeville, Minn.: The Liturgical Press, 1991.

Johnson, Luke T. *The Literary Function of Possessions in Luke-Acts.* Missoula, Mont.: Scholars Press, 1977.

Karris, Robert J. *Luke: Artist and Theologian.* New York: Paulist Press, 1985.

*Malina, Bruce J. and Richard L. Rohrbaugh. *Social-Science Commentary on the Synoptic Gospels.* Minneapolis, Minn.: Fortress Press, 1992.

Neyrey, Jerome, ed. *The Social World of Luke-Acts.* Peabody, Mass.: Hendrickson, 1991. See particularly, John Elliott, "Temple Versus Household in Luke-Acts: A Contrast in Social Institutions," pp. 211-240; Douglas Oakman, "The Countryside in Luke-Acts,"pp. 151-179; John J. Pilch, "Sickness and Healing in Luke-Acts," pp. 181-209.

* Reid, Barbara E., O.P. *A Retreat With Luke: Stepping Out on the Word of God.* Cincinnati: St. Anthony Messenger Press, 2000.

Scott, Bernard Brandon. *Hear Then the Parable.* Minneapolis, Minn.: Augsburg Fortress Press, 1989.

* Weber, Rev. Gerard P., and Rev. Robert L. Miller. *Breaking Open the Gospel of Luke.* Cincinnati: St. Anthony Messenger Press, 1990.

Luke's Gospel and Acts: Feminist Studies

Collins, John N. "Did Luke Intend a Disservice to Women in the Martha and Mary Story?" *Biblical Theology Bulletin* 28.3 (Fall, 1998): pp. 104-111.

Corley, Kathleen E. *Private Women, Public Meals: Social Conflict in the Synoptic Tradition.* Peabody, Mass.: Hendrickson, 1993.

D'Angelo, Mary Rose. "Women in Luke-Acts: A Redactional View." *Journal of Biblical Literature* 109.3 (1990): pp. 441-461.

Evans, Mary J. *Woman in the Bible.* Downers Grove, Ill.: InterVarsity Press, 1983.

* Newsom, Carol A. and Sharon H. Ringe, eds. *The Women's Bible Commentary.* Louisville, Ky.: Westminster John Knox Press, 1992.

Reid, Barbara E. *Choosing the Better Part?: Women in the Gospel of Luke.* Collegeville, Minn.: The Liturgical Press, 1996.

Ringe, Sharon H. *Luke.* Louisville, Ky.: Westminster John Knox Press, 1995.

Schüssler-Fiorenza, Elisabeth. *In Memory of Her: A Feminist Theological Reconstruction of Christian Origins.* New York: Crossroad, 1983.

Torjesen, Karen Jo. *When Women Were Priests.* New York: HarperCollins, 1993.

Women's Psychology and Spirituality

* Conn, Joann Wolski. *Women's Spirituality: Resources for Christian Development.* New York: Paulist Press, 1986. See particularly, Carol Gilligan, "In a Different Voice: Visions of Maturity"; Sandra M. Schneiders, "The Effects of Women's Experience on Their Spirituality."

* ______. *Women's Spirituality: Resources for Christian Development,* 2nd ed. New York: Paulist Press, 1996. See particularly, Joann Wolski Conn, "Restriction and Reconstruction"; Rosemary Haughton, "Women and the Spirituality of Hope and Fear."

Fischer, Kathleen. *Women at the Well: Feminist Perspectives on Spiritual Direction.* New York: Paulist Press, 1988.

Gilligan, Carol. *In a Different Voice: Psychological Theory and Women's Development.* Cambridge, Mass.: Harvard University Press, 1982.

Guenther, Margaret. *Holy Listening: The Art of Spiritual Direction.* Boston: Cowley, 1992.

Johnson, Elizabeth A. *Friends of God and Prophets: A Feminist Theological Reading of the Communion of Saints.* New York: Continuum, 1998.

______. *She Who Is: The Mystery of God in Feminist Theological Discourse.* New York: Crossroad, 1992.

*Kerr, Barbara A. *Smart Girls (Revised Edition): A New Psychology of Girls, Women and Giftedness.* Scottsdale, Ariz.: Gifted Psychology Press, 1997.

*Pipher, Mary. *Reviving Ophelia: Saving the Selves of Adolescent Girls.* New York: Putnam, 1994.

Ruether, Rosemary Radford. *New Woman, New Earth.* New York: Seabury Press, 1975.

Saussy, Carroll. *God Images and Self-Esteem: Empowering Women in a Patriarchal Society.* Louisville, Ky.: Westminster John Knox Press, 1991.

*Winter, Miriam Therese. *WomanWord: A Feminist Lectionary and Psalter: Women of the New Testament.* New York: Crossroad, 1990.

Mary

Jegen, Carol Frances, ed. *Mary According to Women.* Kansas City, Mo.: Sheed and Ward, 1985.

Küng, Hans and Jurgen Moltmann, eds. *Mary in the Churches.* New York: Seabury Press, 1983.

*McBride, Alfred, O. Praem. *Images of Mary.* Cincinnati: St. Anthony Messenger Press, 1999.

*Warner, Marina. *Alone of All Her Sex.* New York: Alfred A. Knopf, 1976.

Anger and Conflict

*Lerner, Harriet Goldhor. *The Dance of Anger: A Woman's Guide to Changing the Patterns of Intimate Relationships.* New York: Harper and Row, 1985.

*Saussy, Carroll. *The Gift of Anger: A Call to Faithful Action.* Louisville: Westminster John Knox Press, 1995.

*Tavis, Carol. *Anger: The Misunderstood Emotion.* New York: Simon and Schuster, 1982.

Women Authors (Literature)

Angelou, Maya. *I Know Why the Caged Bird Sings.* New York: Random House, 1970.

Brontë, Charlotte. *Jane Eyre.* New York: Cambridge University Press, 1996.

Chopin, Kate. *The Awakening.* New York: W. W. Norton, 1994.

Rich, Adrienne. *The Fact of a Doorframe: Poems Selected and New.* New York: W. W. Norton, 1981.

Shields, Carol. *The Stone Diaries.* New York: Penguin Books, 1993.

Tan, Amy. *The Joy Luck Club.* New York: Ballantine, 1989.

Walker, Alice. *In Search of Our Mothers' Gardens: Womanist Prose.* New York: Harcourt, Brace, 1974.

Woolf, Virginia. *A Room of One's Own.* New York: Harcourt, Brace, 1957.

Other Works of Interest

Adler, Mortimer J. *Six Great Ideas.* New York: Macmillan, 1981.

*John Paul II. *Evangelium Vitae* (*The Gospel of Life*). Encyclical Letter. Washington, D.C.: United States Catholic Conference, 1995.

*Nouwen, Henri. *The Inner Voice of Love.* New York: Doubleday, 1996.

* ______. *Lifesigns: Intimacy, Fecundity, and Ecstasy in Christian Perspective.* Garden City, N.Y.: Doubleday, 1986.

Index

84 - PAIN ***
89 alienation to join w Christ in communion w God in creation
94 → sorting truth from falsehood
sorting truth from falsehood - 94-99
Dealing w anger 99-102
100 - ANGER
103 M/W communication styles → 105